How to Carve Bellamy Eagles
Paul B. Rolfe

4880 Lower Valley Road, Atglen, Pennsylvania 19310

Copyright © 2010 by Paul B. Rolfe

Library of Congress Control Number: 2010936364

Designed by Ian Robertson
Type set in Zurich BT

ISBN: 978-0-7643-3572-3
Printed in China

Contents

Introduction
The Golden Age of American Wood Carving

The years from 1790 to 1925 should be considered the Golden Age of American Wood Carving in the United States. During the 1800s, wood carving shops were very common, especially near the shipyards of major ports such as New York and Boston. The carvers worked long hours to keep up with the demand for carved stern boards, figure-heads, and various other architectural ornaments for ships. The work of William Rush (1756-1833) helped set the standard for woodcarvers in the century to follow.

Many woodcarvers of the period found work carving show figures and tobacconist figures. Talented carvers such as Samuel A. Robb (1851-1928) set up shop in New York and enjoyed a thriving business. He also carved phenomenally ornamental circus wagons and displays. He continued carving into the 1920s.

Another niche market was found by sculptors in wood with the now famous names of Dentzel, Mueller, and Illions, among others. The carousel industry was born in Europe, but was celebrated in America where it became a huge industry. A great many of these carvers came from Europe where they were classically trained in the arts. Some carousel machines were very simple and were designed to be broken down and travel across the country while others were very elaborate and stationary, and served as the focal point of many amusement parks. The carousel carving shops grew into factories that employed many carvers, painters, and engineers.

(For a list of publications that feature the woodcarvers of this era, please refer to the bibliography at the end of this book.)

By the turn of the 20th century, technological progress, changing lifestyles, and public opinions put woodcarver's livelihood in jeopardy. Wooden ships were replaced with steel and the demand for carved ornamentation was greatly reduced. Cigar store Indians were losing their popularity and many were being mass-produced out of zinc instead of wood. Many of the figures used as advertisement used de-rogatory racial stereotypes and, though they were considered humor-ous in the 19th century, they were later frowned upon. Sadly, by the 1920s, carousel horses were being made with aluminum and plastic parts. Wood carvers were also being replaced by carving machines that could turn out dozens of pieces at a time. At best, restoration and repair work kept some of the carvers employed. The final nail in the coffin of wood carving as a viable trade in the United States was the Stock Market crash of 1929.

Today, woodcarving is actually viewed by some as being commer-cially worthless. Computer controlled carving machines make it very hard for carvers to compete on a commercial basis. The few individuals who have been able to make a living at woodcarving possess a unique blend of creativity, technical skill, and, most importantly, an ability to find a market willing to pay for their work. Fortunately, the number of carvers that carve just for themselves, their family, and friends, and not for hire, is greater than it ever was.

One of the many talented artists who operated a shop in the glory years of woodcarving was John Haley Bellamy of Kittery Point, Maine. Bellamy was most famous for his carved eagles. These ranged from the small, very light "Portsmouth Eagles" (also known simply as "Bel-lamy Eagles") to the enormous Lancaster Eagle figurehead.

Bellamy's work probably has been copied more than any other 19th century carver. What is it about Bellamy's carvings that inspire so many imitators? I believe that there are two reasons. First, most of his carvings are more than just a maritime carving; they are symbols of American patriotism. And second, they are not so imposing in design or scale to discourage even a novice carver from attempting them.

The purpose of this book is not to produce exacting reproductions of Bellamy's carved eagles, but to instruct carvers how to carve in the style of the original artist. The stylized nature of the eagles make them fun projects for carvers of all skill levels. Since they are not exacting duplicates, you can feel free to add any of your own personal touches. This book is written from the point of view of a carver who admires the design of Bellamy's work as it relates to the efficient execution of carving techniques.

For a historical look at John Bellamy's life and his work, the book, *John Haley Bellamy, Carver of Eagles* by Yvonne Brault Smith is highly recommended. It is available through the Portsmouth Marine Society.

Chapter One

John Haley Bellamy

John Haley Bellamy was born in Kittery Point, Maine on April 16, 1836. As a woodcarver, he is best known for his small eagle plaques and, perhaps the greatest accomplishment of his career, the eagle figurehead that adorned the bow of the USS Lancaster. Throughout his career he worked out of shops in Boston, Massachusetts, Portsmouth, New Hampshire, and at home in Kittery Point. Most of Bellamy's commissions came through the Navy, but he also carved for area businesses and other ship builders.

Bellamy was a man of many talents. He carved other things besides eagles, including animals and ornamentation on frames, furniture, clocks and coats of arms. He was an inventor and held patents on tools and Masonic clock designs. On top of all that, he was also a writer and poet.

A device that Bellamy may have designed for himself was his "Night Slate." It is constructed of a dovetailed walnut box with a hinged pine lid. It contained within it a roll of writing paper, which could be scrolled onto another roll by means of an attached knob. The lid of the box contained a narrow slot with a raised "hump" below it. Bel-

Bellamy's Night Slade. *By permission of the Mariners' Museum, Newport News, Va.*

John Bellamy at approximately 24 years of age. *Courtesy of Farnsworth Art Museum, Rockland, ME.*

Inside view of the Night Slade showing scrolls and extra rolls of paper. *By permission of the Mariners' Museum, Newport News, Va.*

lamy used this device to record thoughts that came to him during the night. Without the benefit of light, Bellamy could reach for the Night Slate with its attached pencil and begin writing on the paper beneath the slot in the lid. When his pencil reached the far right of the slot, he could scroll down to record another line of text. At the time of his death, the paper inside of the Night Slate was found to have recorded a poem in Bellamy's hand.

> There's sharks a lurking in the sea
> There's wolves within the wood
> Buzzards perched on many a tree
> In a carnivorous brotherhood

Bellamy submitted many articles and poems for publication, but this poem definitely reveals some deep, dark thoughts. But what a great idea it was to design such a device that could record inspirations and ideas in the middle of the night when creative minds are not so consumed by the goings on of the day.

Bellamy got his start carving in the shop of Laban Beecher (1805-1876). Beecher is best known for his carving of Andrew Jackson for

Eagle carved by Laban Beecher, one of Bellamy's tutors in his early years as a wood carver. *Courtesy of Farnsworth Art Museum, Rockland, ME.*

the figurehead of the Constitution. Apparently, the work ran out and Bellamy was let go when he was 21 years old. One just has to look at a carving of a small eagle plaque by Beecher to see where the foundation was laid for Bellamy's future as a carver of eagles.

John Bellamy was 25 years old when the Civil War broke out. He took no active part in the war. In the years following his apprenticeship in Beecher's shop, Bellamy studied art, and penmanship. It is this training that led to his career as a talented and creative artist.

Only two photos of any of John Bellamy's shops are known to exist. The shop near his Kittery Point home was located on the upper level of a building overlooking the sea. This shop was known as a local gathering place, where local friends would come and talk while John worked at his bench. Many of his tools, patterns, and carvings have survived and are in the collections of various museums including the Mariners' Museum in Newport News, Virginia, the Farnsworth Art Museum in Rockland Maine, and the Peabody Essex Museum in Salem, Massachusetts.

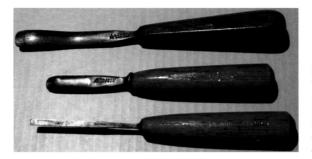

Some of Bellamy's carving tools. Two of them were manufactured by Addis, a popular, good quality brand of the time. *By permission of the Mariners' Museum, Newport News, VA.*

Bellamy developed a distinctive style that was all his own. His "Bellamy Eagle" plaques contained elements that made them identifiable as his work. The stylized simplicity of the design enabled him to complete them very quickly. The carving was not intended to be an accurate depiction of an eagle but a patriotic symbol.

The eagle plaques were constructed of two pieces. Over his bench he kept a wooden template hanging that he used to lay out the 25" long bottom wing section. This base piece was of white pine, just over one inch thick. The sweeping neck and head section was attached with hot hide glue. When finished, these carvings were actually very light and delicate. A "Don't Give Up The Ship" eagle plaque that is in the Mariners' Museum collection weighs just over one pound!

Some of the features that made Bellamy's eagles so distinctive were the shape of the beak and the treatment of the eye. These features and others are found in all of Bellamy eagles.

Bellamy was most productive in the years preceding the creation of the figurehead for the USS *Lancaster* in 1881. The Lancaster eagle

One of only two known photographs of Bellamy's Kittery Point loft shop. A range of styles of eagles are shown. *Courtesy of Farnsworth Art Museum, Rockland, ME.*

Bellamy's magnificent Lancaster Eagle in its restored gold leaf finish. *By permission of the Mariners' Museum of Newport News, Va.*

Bellamy's eagle mounted on the bow of the USS *Lancaster*. It is unknown how long the original gold leaf finish lasted but it is shown here with a two tone painted finish. *Courtesy of the Mariners' Museum, Newport News, Va.*

During the restoration process, many joints had to be repaired. *Courtesy of the Mariners' Museum, Newport News, Va.*

Back view of the eagle during the restoration process. This photo was taken in the original indoor gallery before it was moved to its current location at the Mariners' Museum. *Courtesy of the Mariners' Museum, Newport News, Va.*

was, without a doubt, the crowning achievement of his career. He worked in a loft at the Portsmouth Naval yard for a tradesman's wage of $2.32 a day.

The Lancaster Eagle has a wingspan of nineteen feet and weighs over 3200 pounds. It is almost thirteen feet from beak to tail.

When Bellamy's magnificent eagle was finally removed from the bow of the Lancaster in 1921, it was still in good shape. It was stored outside at the Boston Naval Yard where it began to deteriorate. Efforts to restore it and put it on display were deemed too expensive. Four years later, it was bought for $262.89 by a ship chandler's junk shop. It remained in the shop until 1934 when it was purchased by the Mariners' Museum of Newport News, Virginia, for the sum of $2200.

The huge wings were removed during transport to the Mariners' Museum to avoid any further damage to the carving. Once at its new home, it was reassembled and put on display outside. In 1936, the eagle was brought inside and then, sometime in the 1960s, it was restored to its original brilliant gold leaf finish. Before leafing, the outer surface of the eagle required some repair. All of the glue joints showed some signs of separation and had to be filled. A receipt on file in the Mariners' Museum shows that the cost of the gold leaf was a mere $700 and the labor to apply it was only $300.

As a wood carver, creating a piece of the magnitude of the Lancaster Eagle intrigues me. I was curious as to how Bellamy actually constructed the eagle. I learned a great deal on a visit to the Mariners' Museum, where the staff was very kind and accommodating. This sculpture is a cherished part of their vast maritime collection and they allowed me to take some "behind the scenes" pictures of it. From

A current back view of the Lancaster eagle showing the metal plate that is mounted on the back of the eagle. It is curious that the metal brackets on the left side are attached with a dovetail joint where the ones on the right side are simply bolted down. It must have something to do with the process by which the eagle was assembled on the bow of the ship. *By permission of the Mariners' Museum, Newport News, Va.*

Steel cables stretched between the wings to offer support. Note the gouged out area. *By permission of the Mariners' Museum, Newport News, Va.*

The wing tips are beveled. Was this to allow the carving to fit up against the ship better or as a device to make the wing feathers appear thinner? *By permission of the Mariners' Museum, Newport News, Va.*

behind, you can see some of the construction techniques that I was so curious about.

The body is hollow and made up of who knows how many laminated pieces of white pine. The wings are also laminated and bolted to the body. There is a large metal plate bolted to the top of the body between the wings and four huge L-braces that attach to it and then extend upward along the curved top surface of the wings. Each board that Bellamy used to construct the wings is visible form this perspective. The huge wings are further supported to each other by steel cables that extend between them.

There are some curious hollowed out places on the top of the wings that were obviously excavated with carving tools. We can only imagine that Bellamy found out at the last minute that they were necessary to accommodate some feature of the ship's bow so that the eagle could snuggle up tightly. Another carving detail of note is the beveling of the tips of the wing feathers. They may have actually served two purposes: making the wing tips appear thinner and simply matching the contour of the ship.

Bellamy's treatment of the tail feathers seems odd when taken out of context. They are split into two separate halves. They make

This eagle appears to have two sets of tail feathers. It was never meant to be seen this way. *By permission of the Mariners' Museum, Newport News, Va.*

The back view shows how the tail was constructed. The unfinished joinery is in contrast to the finely gilded finish of the other side. *By permission of the Mariners' Museum, Newport News, Va.*

much more sense when you see the eagle mounted on the bow of the ship.

An amazing feature of the Lancaster eagle is the contrast seen between the outer and inner surfaces of the wings and tail feathers. The outer surfaces show the finely carved details in restored gold leaf. The inner surfaces, which were originally up against the bow of the ship, show the crude laminations of every piece of wood that Bellamy used and made no attempt to hide.

Bellamy Eagles For Sale

John Bellamy did not live an extravagant life. He was a tradesman who served a flourishing industry that became obsolete during his lifetime. His work provided him with a comfortable life up to the end, when the work stopped and the money began to run out. He made many of the small eagles that he is known for to give as gifts, for trade,

"Don't Give Up The Ship" seems to be the most often used slogan by Bellamy. Painted pine, 25" long. $145,000 *Courtesy of Northeast Auctions, Portsmouth, NH.*

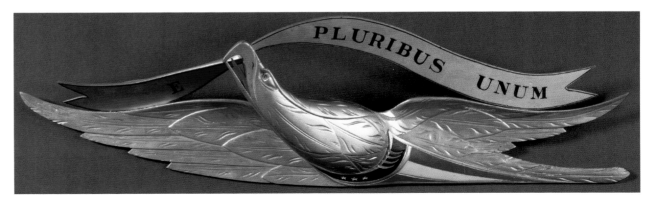

Bellamy used banners and flags in many different ways. *Courtesy of Northeast Auctions, Portsmouth, NH.* $17,400

This 48" long eagle holds the record for the highest successful auction bid for a Bellamy eagle. $600,000 *Courtesy of Northeast Auctions, Portsmouth, NH*

or for a day's wage of just $2.50. It is one of the sad ironies of life that the true value of a craftsman's or artist's work is not realized until long after they have passed.

The small eagle plaque with the banner that reads, "Don't Give Up The Ship" was a very popular one for Bellamy. There have been more eagles with that theme than any others that have come up for auction. In 2005, one such eagle, which was painted white, was sold to the highest bidder for $145,000. A variation of the common 25-inch long plaque that had a banner without the staff that read "E PLURIBUS UNUM" sold for $17,400 at auction in August, 2006.

One of Bellamy's more elaborate eagle plaques measured 48 inches long and has a banner that reads "GOD IS OUR REFUGE AND STRENGTH" . The eagle's finely carved talons are holding a shield and two crossed flags. The piece is assembled from several separately carved parts. It sold for a record $600,000 at a New Hampshire auction in August, 2005. A similar although much smaller carving sold for $101,500 in August, 2007.

The eagle that we will carve in Chapter 12 of this book is based the Bellamy eagle shown here. This design is a departure from his typical plaques. It sold for $12,360 at auction in August, 2005.

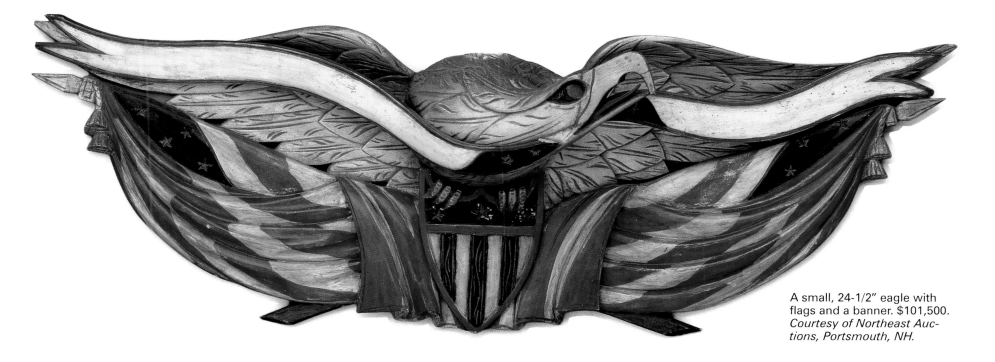

A small, 24-1/2" eagle with flags and a banner. $101,500. *Courtesy of Northeast Auctions, Portsmouth, NH.*

A different style of eagle carved by Bellamy. 21" long. $12,360. *Courtesy of James D. Julia, Inc., Fairfield ME, www.jamesjulia.com.*

A pilot house eagle that was attributed to Bellamy went up for auction in 2004 with an expected high estimate of $30,000, but did not sell. This eagle was part of the inspiration that led to the design of the eagle that we will carve in Chapter 8.

It is obvious that there has been a tremendous amount of collector interest in Bellamy eagles. Between the years of 1998 and 2009 numerous Bellamy eagles were sold at auction for a total of more than 2.3 million dollars. Would John Bellamy have believed it, back in the year 1900, if someone told him that his work would some day be so sought after by collectors and museums one hundred years later? Will the value of his work continue to rise?

The last known photograph of Bellamy at approximately 64 years old. Taken near his shop in Kittery Point. *Courtesy of Farnsworth Art Museum, Rockland, ME.*

A pilot house eagle attributed to John Bellamy. 23" tall. *Courtesy of Pook & Pook, Inc., Downingtown, PA.*

Chapter Two

In The Shop

Woodcarving tools are stored in a rolling chest with drawers.

Wood carving is no different than any other craft in that you need tools to work with and a place to work. Woodcarving tools can vary from a simple knife and your lap to a collection of hundreds of gouges and chisels and a sturdy workbench in a well equipped workshop.

For the projects shown in this book, the style of woodcarving is very traditional, with the work piece secured to a workbench by means of clamps or held in a vise. This frees up both hands so that the gouges can either be held with two hands or driven with a mallet.

The Tools

Almost all of the gouges and chisels used in the projects in this book are of European manufacture. The Europeans have been making woodcarving tools for centuries; they know how to do it right. In Bellamy's era, there were a few tool manufacturers in the United States. Those domestic tools that were available then are no longer being made of the same quality now. The woodcarving tool market suffered in the U.S. with the decline of the woodcarving industry in the 1930s.

Up until the 1970s, woodcarving tools were not as "refined" as they are today. They often did not come with handles, the steel was not polished and the edges had only the factory bevel on them. They were as sharp as screwdrivers! The professional carvers often preferred them that way so that they could sharpen them in the manner that best suited their particular application.

When the woodcarving hobby scene exploded in the United States in the 1970s and 1980s, a new demand was put on the woodcarving tool manufacturers. Now, carvers insist that the tools be ready to use

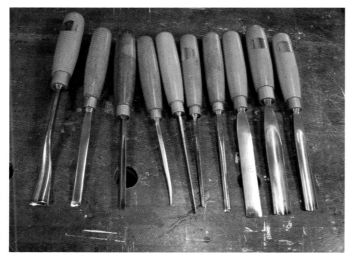

Carving tools made by Ashley Iles. When laid out together, they all look alike at first glance.

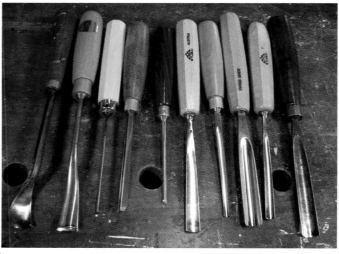

Carving tools of different vintage and manufacture offer a way to pick out certain tools.

right off the shelf. They have to come with handles; they have to look good on the shelf so they are all polished; and, most importantly, they have to be sharp. Competition between the companies insures that these demands are met. Unfortunately, these extra steps in the manufacturing process result in tools that are more expensive.

To the new carver about to start purchasing woodcarving tools, I have three recommendations. Number One: Always buy the best quality tools that you can afford. "You get what you pay for" definitely applies here. Number Two: Do not be tempted to buy a large set of tools. Sets of carving tools are assembled by the manufacturers and distributors based on what they think will sell. They are well meaning and often the set will have a good mix of tools, but there may be tools in that set that you may not need right away, or the set may have the right shapes for you but they are the wrong size for what you are doing. For example, a lot of sets will contain one or two chisels in them. This is not necessarily a bad thing, but unless you are doing lettering with the tools, you might not need them at first. They are put in the set because they are inexpensive to make so they keep the price of the set down.

Number Three: Don't buy all the same brand of tools. During the carving process, you will probably have a dozen or so tools laid out on the bench in front of you. If they are all the same brand, they will all look alike at first glance. If, on the other hand, your tools are from many different manufacturers, the particular tool that you need at a precise moment will probably be easier to find. This makes the carving process a lot more efficient. I use some vintage tools, as well, which makes them stand out from the others when they are needed.

Urethane coated mallet, leather covered mallet, and drawknives of different sizes.

The only disadvantage of mixing brands of tools is that there are, unfortunately, manufacturers that do not follow the most widely used Sheffield numbering system for their tools. This means that, for example, a #3 gouge in one brand will not be the identical sweep as the same width #3 gouge of another brand. This is not necessarily a bad thing as long as you are aware of it. The underlying issue here is that the Sheffield system of numbering the various sweeps of carving tools was intended to make the tool shapes follow a standard system and thus make communication and documentation of the woodcarving process easier to follow and understand.

The first tools that you purchase should include a deep gouge, a medium gouge, and a shallow gouge. You should also get a v-tool and a good knife. The width of the tools you buy is determined by the scale of the work that you are doing. For a lot of medium size projects, about 3/8" to 1/2" (10 mm to 12 mm) are good starting widths. Stick to a European brand of tools and you cannot go wrong.

The best way for you to add to your tool collection is to simply start carving and let your particular job requirements determine which tools that you need to buy next. Another thing to keep in mind is that there are hundreds and hundreds of variations of professional or full-size tools. There are also an infinite number of curves in nature and they are always changing. Therefore, there is no such thing as a required list of tools that you absolutely must have. Be flexible.

Other tools that you will need for the projects in this book are a drawknife or two and a good mallet. Traditionally, wooden mallets of apple, hard maple, or lignum vitae were used. I prefer the modern urethane coated variety that are available today. One of my favorite mallets, although it is not very practical for heavy work, is one that I made with leather, by gluing layers of leather discs over a lignum vitae core. The lignum vitae core was an older mallet that was cracked and I did not use much. I turned it on the lathe so that it was shaped like two straight cylinders. After stacking and gluing the leather layers on the core, it was mounted in the lathe again and turned to its final shape. The mallet has cocobolo caps on each end and another piece that separates the handle from the business end of the mallet. It really feels good in my hand

The Workbench

A sturdy workbench is a must-have item for a traditional woodcarving shop. There are several versions available commercially, but one that you make yourself is almost always better. The bench should

Emmert pattern makers vise mounted on workbench.

Emmert vise fixed in a lifted, twisted, and tapered position.

Second workbench with tool chest underneath.

have a couple of vises and holes for dogs. The heavier the bench the better. My main workbench has a 3" thick cherry top.

The vise shown in the photo is an Emmert Pattern Makers vise. This particular model was manufactured around 1900 and is positively the ultimate woodworking vise. It is 18 inches long and opens up over 14 inches! It will rotate 360 degrees and tilt up to any angle towards workbench surface. The jaws will adjust to a slight angle to hold objects that are irregularly shaped. These vises are becoming rare and, as a result, expensive. There is an imported vise currently available which is a copy of a later model Emmert available, but it is not near the quality of an original. You will see this vise in action later in this book when we are carving the Pilot House Eagle.

Over time, you will accumulate a collection of tools and you will need a place to store them. Some carvers like to hang their tools in a wall cabinet near their workbench. This is good because you can see all the tools at once, which makes it easy to find the one that you're after. I chose instead to make a cabinet with drawers to store my carving tools. This allows me to take them all to a show if I need them for demonstrations. It is also located right next to the door of the shop so that if there ever was a fire, it would be the first thing out.

The power arm work positioner is an excellent way to hold in-the-round carvings. It will rotate and tilt your work piece securely in many different positions so that you can carve it from every conceivable angle.

Power arm work positioner for in-the-round carvings.

Arkansas stone, ultra fine black Arkansas stone, honing oil, slip stones, and leather strop.

Tool Sharpening

Sharpening woodcarving tools has always been a challenging task to master. I believe that it is important to learn how to sharpen by hand before you attempt to use a machine. I have always used oil stones to establish the correct bevel and a leather strop to polish the edge. You can use oil stones, water stones, diamond stones, ceramic stones, or even sandpaper to sharpen your tools; it really doesn't matter. What matters is the technique that you use.

For practical reasons, a spinning leather, felt, or composite wheel that is charged with an abrasive compound is most often used to maintain the edge on the tools. Eventually though, you will have to go back to the stones to re-establish the proper bevel. The Tormek® sharpening system does a very good job honing the edges of carving tools. It will also sharpen practically any edged tool under the sun. It is shown here set up to sharpen a drawknife, which is a difficult tool to get a good edge on; this machine makes it easy. What makes the Tormek® system so good is that it takes the human element out of the sharpening process. The tool is held at a constant angle with a jig so that an accurate bevel is maintained throughout the sharpening process. It uses a water-cooled stone so that it is impossible to overheat the tool. The effective grit of the stone can be changed and there is a leather wheel that will provide a perfectly honed edge.

Other tools

There are many other shop tools that are good to have. A good band saw is almost imperative. For the projects in this book, I also used a table saw, a drill press, a router table, a jointer, and a surface planer for stock preparation.

This mahogany Bellamy eagle was designed to be outside.

Tormek® Sharpening System.

Sharpening a drawknife on the water cooled stone. The grit of the stone can be changed from 220 grit to 1000 grit by using a stone grader. The leather wheel has a grit of 6000 when the honing compound is applied.

Honing the edge of the drawknife on the leather wheel.

Materials

Before you begin carving any of the projects in this book, there are a couple of things to consider. First, do you have the tools and materials that are necessary to complete to job? Remember that you don't need to have the exact tools that are shown here, but you should have some that are similar.

Most of the projects shown in this book were carved out of basswood. You don't have to use basswood; use whatever wood you have that is suitable. You can also change the dimensions to accommodate the wood that you have. Most of the Bellamy Eagles were painted and ours will be no different, so basswood is perfect. Bellamy used a lot of white pine for his eagles. Good quality white pine is regional and may be harder to find than the more commonly available basswood. Mahogany is a very good carving wood and makes for a very attractive eagle. It is too attractive to paint so just finish it naturally with an appropriate finish. If your eagle is to be displayed outside, be sure to use glue that is waterproof.

Warning: Please note that some of the tools used and techniques employed in this book are potentially dangerous. Be sure to understand these dangers, especially those associated with the use of power tools. In some of the photographs contained in this text, guards have been removed and band saw upper blade guides have been raised for photographic purposes. Use common sense and do not work when you are tired or in a hurry. Don't forget to use safety glasses and dust collection.

Chapter Three
Carving a Bellamy Style Eagle

The thing that makes this such a fun project to carve is that it is so stylized that it can be carved very quickly. Bellamy, an accomplished professional, would have been able to carve one of his 25-inch long eagles in a few hours. To make the production even faster, he would have sawn out several heads and bodies at the same time. He probably had some of these parts partially roughed out so that when he received an order for an eagle, the turnaround would have been greatly reduced. In many cases, the heads were interchangeable for different body styles. This is the advantage of establishing a distinct pattern. The eagle was customized for the particular recipient by simply adding an applicable message on the banner.

The eagle that we will carve in the next few chapters is slightly larger and heavier than the typical Bellamy eagle. This design is what is often described as Bellamy's "Portsmouth Eagle". It will be constructed from two pieces of high quality northern basswood. The main body and wings are sawn from a piece that is 2" x 6" x 36" long. The head is sawn from a 3" x 6" x 12" long block.

The two parts are sawn out on the band saw. Be sure to take all safety precautions when operating woodworking machinery. I have carved enough of these eagles that it was worth my time to make some patterns out of 1/4" plywood. On the body/wings pattern, I have two drilled small holes that mark the location of some screw holes that will be drilled through the backer board. On the head pattern, I have drilled some holes that will allow me to mark the head blank for areas that will become the open parts of the beak.

During the carving process, the body/wings section will be attached to a backer board with two screws. The screws will pass through the backer board from underneath into the underside of the blank. The location of these screws is marked using the plywood pattern. Whether or not you use a plywood pattern, locate these screws so that they will enter the blank where the wood will remain thick throughout the carving process. You do not want to run into one of the mounting screws with a sharp gouge.

The head blank is sawn from the top view as well as the profile. This will allow the carved head to lift off of the body. Before you saw the top profile though, drill holes that will become the open space of the beak.

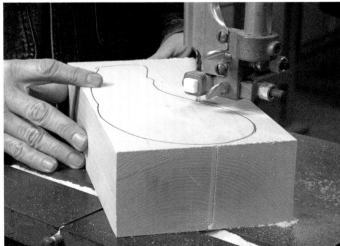

Bandsaw out the head and body/wings.

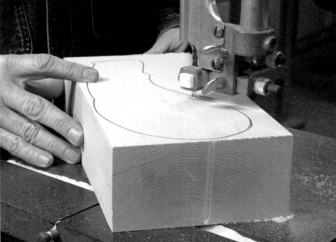

The patterns and basswood blanks.

There are some options to consider for attaching the head to the body. For the eagle project in this book, we will orient the head in the 10 o'clock position. One thing to consider when deciding how to position the head on your carving is where the eagle may eventually be located. For example, if your eagle is to be mounted over a door, consider positioning the head in the 8 o'clock position so that the eagle will appear to be watching you as you walk under it. For the most part, Bellamy positioned the head on his eagles in the 10 o'clock position.

You could even orient your head towards the 3 or 4 o'clock position. If you do this however, you need to saw out the head differently from the side profile.

Lay the head blank on top of the body/wings part in the position that you have decided to carve it and mark around it with a pencil. Also mark three to four indexing marks across the head and the body. These lines will help you to put the head on the body in the same exact place each time you want to check your progress.

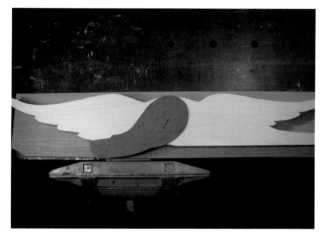

Head in eight o'clock position.

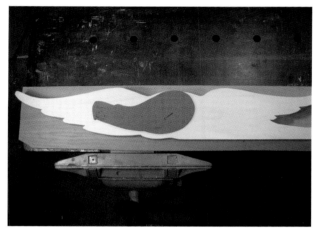

Head in nine o'clock position.

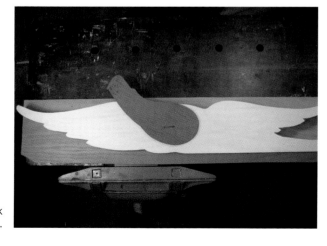

Head in ten o'clock position.

Mark the location of head on the body.

Chapter 4
Carving the Wings

In this chapter, we will carve the long piece of basswood that will become the body and wings of the eagle. I have seen where some carvers use a one-inch thick piece of wood here and glue on pieces for the top of the wings. If you only have thin basswood, this will work, but I prefer to use a two inch thick piece. This just seems easier to me and it allows for more modeling of the carving. There is a lot of waste to remove, but I enjoy this work. It goes by quickly.

The best way to carve off the waste is in a standing position. You can carve much more efficiently this way. If your posterior is planted in a chair, you cannot generate any power from your body to carve. The work is being done by your arms only, so they will get tired quickly. Your arms may still get tired, even if you are standing and moving your body. When this happens, simply hold the gouge in your other hand and swing the mallet with the opposite one.

I have used a power tool before to remove the bulk of the waste from the wings, but I still prefer using gouges and a mallet on these small eagles.

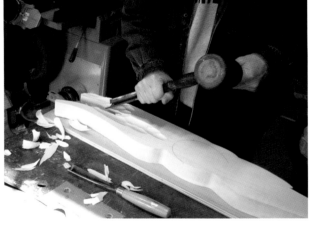

Start roughing out with large gouge.

The tip of wing is worked down to one inch thick – the rest should be about 1/2".

Begin at the ends and work your way toward center.

The tail is also worked down to 1/2".

Start to define the top edge of the shield.

The bottom edge of shield is worked down to 1/2".

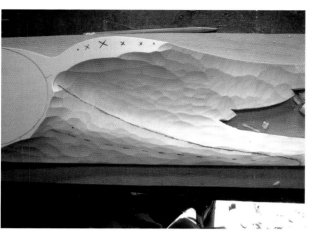

Xes mark the high spot on the wing.

The top of the wing is the highest spot on this part of the carving. This is where some carvers glue on another piece of wood to achieve this height. The largest X marks the spot of the highest spot and the wood marked by the smaller Xes falls away. Draw a dotted line on what is to become the middle of the shield. The shield will be at its highest along this line.

Remember that there is a screw located somewhere under the surface in this region. It may be a comfort to find out and mark exactly where it is. The plywood pattern that was used to layout the body/wing piece has holes in it where these screws were driven up through the backer board. This is when we make use of one of those holes by shining a light through it onto the wood.

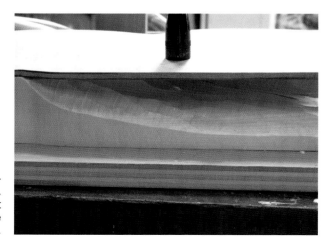

Align the plywood pattern on top of the carving. Place a small flashlight over the location of the screw hole.

The light marks the location of the screw.

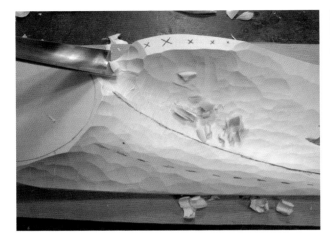

Separate the shoulder from the neck.

Carve under the shoulder to create a shadow.

Round over the shoulder.

We are going to leave the left wing for now and focus on the right wing. The right wing has to be carved to completion before the head is glued on since in will be too hard to get to afterwards. The shaping of this wing goes very quickly because there is no shield on this side.

We will come back to carving the details on the right wing, but first we need to do some more rough shaping of the wings. Unclamp the backer board from the workbench and temporarily remove the screws holding the eagle. Clamp the body/wings in a vise so that the top of the wings are accessible. You may want to use a scrap piece of wood over the flat spot where the head will be attached to protect it from the jaws of the vise.

Smooth out wood on wing

Check bottom edge of shield.

The final shape of the left wing. The talons and the shield center line are sketched in.

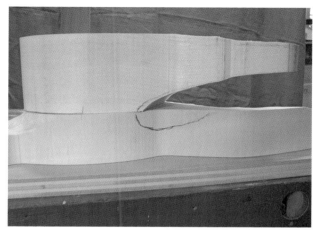

Draw in the transition curve between neck and right wing.

Check location of head.

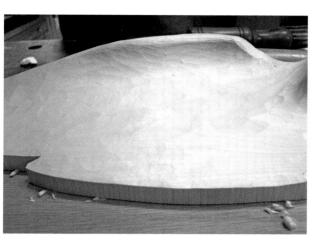

Right wing is shaped and smoothed out.

When your eagle is complete and hanging on a wall, you want the wings to appear like they are no longer just a block of wood with the front side carved. You want the wings to lift off of the wall at the top and tip of the wing. We are going to use a drawknife to carve the back-side of the upper part of the wings. You could use a large flat gouge also. Roughly follow the contour that is on the front side of the wings. While you have the eagle clamped in this position, carve off the band saw marks from the top edges. Turn the eagle over and remove the band saw marks along the bottom edges, too. It is imperative that all of the band saw marks are removed.

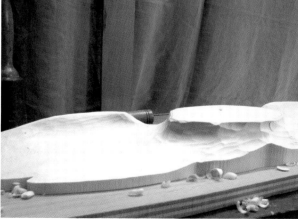

The right wing. Note neck elevation.

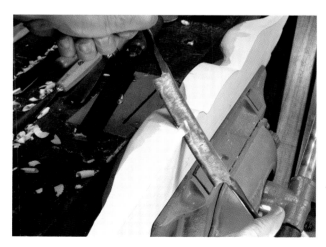

Bevel back side top of wings with draw knife.

Draw feathers
on right wing.

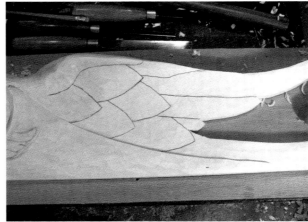

Draw feathers on
left wing.

With the body/wings reattached on the backer board, we can finish carving the right wing. Draw the feathers on both wings as shown on the pattern. These do not have to be exact. This part of the design reflect Bellamy's marketing brilliance. By minimizing the number and the detail found on the feathers, he easily could carve one of these eagles in one day. On the left wing, the top edge of the shield is defined with a v-tool.

On the right wing, start carving the feathers by outlining them with a v-tool. After outlining all of the feathers use a #3 gouge to remove the wood up to these cuts. Repeat this process, if necessary, so that each feather is raised about 1/8" creating a shingled effect. A skewed gouge or chisel helps in the corners. Ideally, the feathers should be slightly crowned.

The transition from the wing to the body and eventually to the head will end up being a U shape. This will take some work, but will be easier to see if you put the head in its place.

Start carving on lines with V-tool.

The feathers on the right wing.

Right wing feathers ready for details.

Draw in the center quill with double line.

Carve on quill lines with V-tool.

Now its time to carve the feather details. Draw the center quill on each feather and carve on this line with a v-tool. The center quill is not completely raised from the surface but is just outlined. The barbs are simple S curves that are carved in pairs. Make these as random as possible. The right wing is now finished!

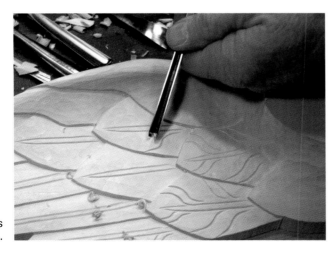

Carve the barbs as pairs of S-curves.

The completed right wing.

The completed left wing.

You can carve the details on the left wing now or, as I did in this example, after the head is attached. The left wing is carved in the same manner as the right wing. Use a v-tool to carve the lines on the shield. These lines will make painting the shield easier. The bottom edge of the shield is defined with a v-tool cut.

On Bellamy's eagles, the talons were carved in many different ways. Some were carved in high detail while others were just outlined with a v-tool cut. Carve the talons on your eagle in a manner that appeals to you. There is no wrong way to carve them.

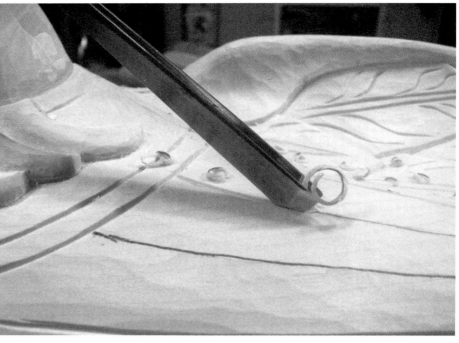

Carve on the design lines of the shield with V-tool.

The simply shaped talons.

Chapter 5
Carving The Head

Some of the carving work on the head must be done before it is attached to the body. The back side is carved first. It is easier to carve this area by hand using a knife. There is no eye carved on the back side and the open beak and tongue are only roughed in. Once again, be sure to remove all of the band saw marks.

Attach the head to its own backer board with screws that extend at least two inches in the head. Draw the eye, beak and tongue details. With the backer board clamped to the workbench, use a coping saw to cut out the open spaces above and below the tongue. Use the holes that were drilled as described in Chapter 3.

After you have carved the back of the head you have two options as to how to proceed with carving the rest of it. You may glue it onto the body now and carve it in place or you can do most of the shaping and some of the details while it is attached to the backer board.

If you glue it on now, the head still has square edges that make it very easy to apply clamps while the glue dries. Clamping the head

Attach head to backer board and draw in details.

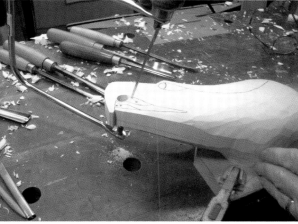

Use a coping saw to cut out spaces in beak.

As an alternate, glue on head first.

Roughing out head.

Smoothing out head to neck.

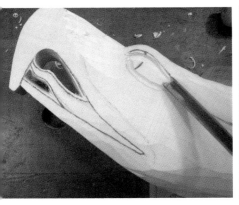
Start carving the eye with V-tool.

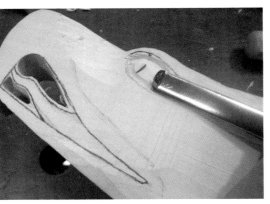
Round over eye with inverted gouge.

Carve dished out pupil.

Shape the tongue.

this way results in a nearly invisible glue line, provided that the surfaces are very flat. The four eagles with their heads being glued on are from a class that I taught on Carving Bellamy Style Eagles at John C Campbell Folk School in Brasstown, North Carolina.

The illustrations that follow show the head being carved while it is attached to the backer board. You may do it either way but I actually prefer to glue it on first.

To rough out the head, start with a medium sweep gouge to remove the bulk of the wood. Smooth the rough texture and round out the base of the head with a large #3 gouge. As with the wings, you may also used a power tool here to remove the waste.

The eye is a bullet shape that tapers at one end and has a concave cup for the pupil at the other end. It is carved by outlining it first with a v-tool and rounding it with an inverted #5 gouge. This process is repeated until the eye is totally convex with no flat spots. The brow

above the eye should be rounded and it should extend out over the eye. The brow line continues off the tapered end of the eye and extends backward on the head. It will eventually become a large feather.

The dished out pupil is carved with a 10 mm #7 gouge. This cut needs to be deep, so that the pupil ends up being nearly round. Carve the beak out in front of the eye, so that it can be seen from a frontal view. You will need a knife or a very sharp skew chisel to clean out the corner of the eye.

Start defining the tongue with a v-tool and then shape it with a knife and some skewed gouges. The lower part of the beak tapers towards its end and is rounded on the bottom. The upper part of the beak has square corners in keeping with the Bellamy style.

Use a v-tool to carve in the separation of the head from the hard part of the beak. Then use a #3 gouge to carve down the hard part of the beak. Soften all of the edges and clean up all of the rough cuts.

Add details to beak.

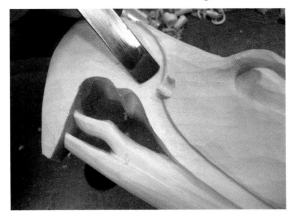
Smooth beak with # 3 gouge.

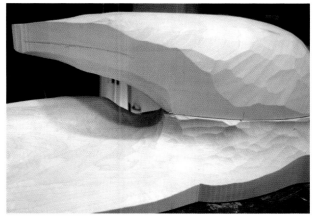

Check head alignment one last time.

Apply glue to both surfaces.

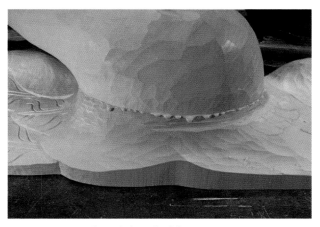

Attach head with screws.

Before you glue on the head, put it in place on the body temporarily. Line up the indexing marks to make sure that it is in the right place. You will find that there are places where some wood could be removed to make the transition flow better. Pay particular attention to the area under the neck that will be harder to access after the head is glued on. If the mating surfaces do not come together seamlessly, correct them now to get a good joint.

Drill two 3/16" pilot holes through the body and countersink them from the backside. Spread glue on both surfaces and draw the two pieces together with 3" screws. The glue should be allowed to dry overnight before proceeding with the carving.

After the glue has dried, the process of blending in the two parts begins. Use a #9 gouge to clean up under the head and flatter gouges everywhere else.

A v-tool is used to define the top edge of the shield. The edge of the shield should be made continuous around all of its edges. If it suits you, you may carve a couple of small stars on the upper portion of the shield.

A large #3 gouge is used to carve down the sides of the head and blend it in to the body. The head should taper down gently to the body and there should be no flat spots left of the head. As a general rule, you should not leave machined or original surfaces on any carving, whether it is in relief or in the round.

Define top of shield.

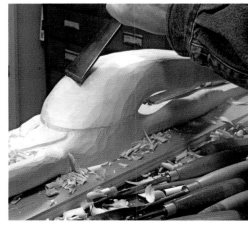

Final smoothing of head and neck.

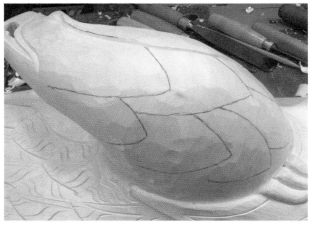

Draw feathers on head.

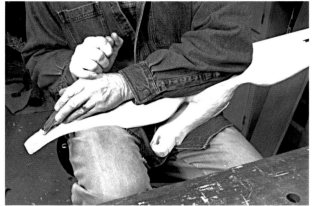

Carve back side of wing tips.

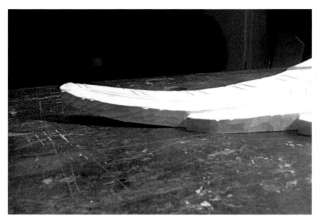

The "lift" of the wing tips.

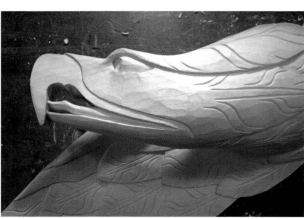

Head and neck detail.

Draw out the feathers on the head. One large feather originates at the eye and continues across the top of the head. You can play with the number and size of the feathers but just make sure that they all point in the same direction. The feathers are carved in the same manner as the ones on the wings.

Remove the eagle from the backer board and take off some wood from the back of the wing tips. This will give them some lift when the eagle is mounted on a wall. You may use a gouge as shown here or a knife.

The carving of the main part of the eagle is now complete. If you plan on adding a banner, proceed to the next chapter.

Here are some pictures of the completed eagle.

Finished eagle.

Head detail.

Talons close up.

Head and neck.

Chapter Six
Making The Banner

The banner was a very important part of Bellamy's eagles. The banners gave the eagle a patriotic theme with painted messages such as "Don't Give Up The Ship," Live Free Or Die," or *Dum Vivimus Vivamus*" ("While we Live, Let us Live"). Other non-patriotic messages included "Merry Christmas" and "Happy New Year." It is with these banners that Bellamy could give his eagles a personal touch, thus broadening their appeal.

This is your chance to personalize your eagle, as well. Use a patriotic slogan or a phrase that has some special meaning to you or the person who will eventually receive your carving.

The banner is made in two pieces, the flag and the staff. You may use either basswood or pine. Use the pattern to draw out the outline of the flag on a piece of stock that is 8" x 32" x 3/4". The staff starts out as a piece of square stock that is 3/4" x 3/4" x 32". Use the band saw to cut out the shape of the flag.

A spoke shave makes quick work of removing all of the band saw marks from the edge of the flag.

The two parts of the banner are joined with a lap joint. In order to obtain a good joint, the parts must be machined accurately. It is imperative that the flat end of the flag is straight and very close to the angle as drawn on the pattern. The rabbet joint is registered from this surface. A 12" disc sander is the perfect tool to get a good machined edge here.

Use either a table saw or a router to machine a rabbet that measures 3/4" long and 3/8" deep on the underside of the straight edge of the flag.

For the staff, machine a piece of basswood or pine to 3/4" x 3/4" x 32" long. Overlay the rabbet on the flag onto the staff approximately 5 inches from one end and mark its position on the staff with a pencil. At this point, you should

Saw out banner on bandsaw.

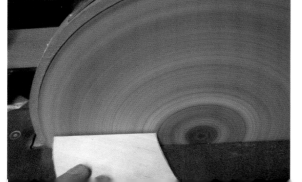

Sand end of banner with disc sander.

Remove bandsaw marks with spokeshave.

Lap joints for banner and staff.

Cutting joint in staff on table saw.

Assemble joint without glue.

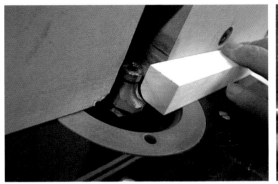
Round over staff on router table.

Remove machine marks with back-bent gouge.

temporarily clamp the two pieces together and lay them on the carved eagle. The flag/staff should rest on the eagle as seen in one of the photographs in this book that show the completed assembly. If the angle that is formed by the banner and the staff is either too large or too small, it may be adjusted by altering the end of the flag on the disc sander. The rabbet will have to be re-cut also.

A table saw is used to cut a 3/8" deep recess in the staff. The saw blade will cut the edges of the recess at 90 degrees to the staff. Since the banner is to be joined to the staff at an angle, adjustments to the edges of the recess must be made with a chisel so that the two pieces fit together. Dry fit them together, but do not glue them at this time.

On the top end of the staff, cut a pointed spire and either carve or sand off the machine marks.

The staff is rounded below the point where the banner is joined. A roundover bit in a router is used to do most of the work of shaping the staff from square to round. A back bent gouge is used to remove the machine marks and add carved facets. A knife could be used here also. Do not round over the staff where it joins with the banner or else there will be a gap there.

Lay the dry-fitted banner assembly on top of the carved eagle. Note the three pencils in the photo. They mark the locations where the banner and the staff are to be attached to the eagle. Screws will be countersunk from the back of the eagle to attach the flag and staff at the two locations on the left. On the right side, the banner appears to rest on the top edge of the eagle's wing. It will be attached here with a metal bracket from behind. We are getting close, but there is still a little bit of carving to do.

Pencils show where banner is joined with the eagle.

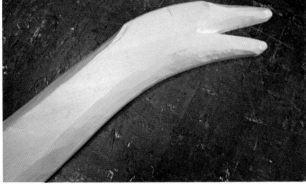
Bevel back side of banner, leave a flat spot for attaching bracket.

Assembled banner and staff. Note details on staff end.

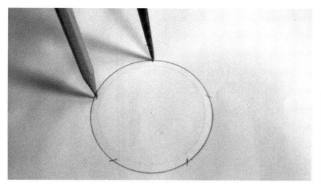

Draw circle with compass and add five equally spaced marks.

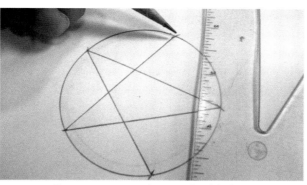

Connect every other mark with line.

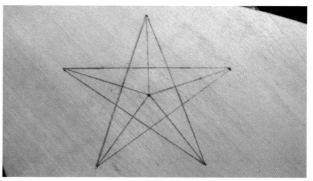

Drawn star with five center lines that meet in the center.

The back side of the banner is beveled so that it will not appear too thick when viewed from the front. Bevel back about one inch and leave about 1/4" on the outside edge. (On an original Bellamy eagle, the banner was only 3/8" thick and beveled to about 1/8" from the top edge. I think that this is a very fragile design and, in fact, on the Bellamy eagle in the Mariners' Museum's collection, the banner was broken and repaired due to weak cross grain on the banner.) Do not bevel the banner where the metal bracket will be attached later to join it to the eagle's wing.

There is some carved decoration on the end of the staff just to dress it up. Sand the edges and the front surface of the banner up to P220 grit.

There was a carved star on many of Bellamy's banners so we will carve one on ours also. Carving a star is very simple and requires only a couple of chisels. We begin by drawing a circle that is as big as you want the star tips to reach. It turns out to be about 2-1/2" in diameter here. There are mathematical formulas in texts that show you how to lay out a perfect star, but this method works just fine without the numbers. Start at a point on the circle and mark off five equal divisions with a compass. This will take some trial and error of adjusting the compass until you get it just right. Mark those five points on the circle. These points will become the points of the star. To complete the drawing, connect every other mark together with a line. Finally, draw a line from each point to the center of the star. The center is where the compass point was when the original circle was drawn. These lines will become the bottom of the vee of each leg. It is this crisp line that gives a carved star a very clean, distinctive look.

Begin the carving process by driving a carving chisel (beveled on both sides) along the center line at a slight angle. The cut is deeper at the center and slants out of the wood at the tip of the leg. Use a wide

Cut center line with chisel.

Cut down to center line with a skew chisel.

Clean up the bottom.

The finished star.

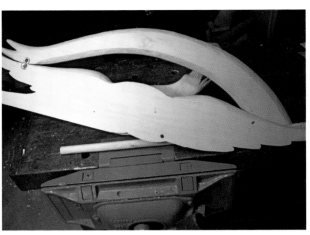

Rear view showing attachment points.

Bracket that attaches banner to top of left wing.

skew chisel to gut out triangular slivers of wood. Work your way from the center line out to the outer line of the leg. The finished cut will result in a plane that ends at the bottom of the leg.

When all of the legs have been carved, they should all meet at the bottom at the center point of the star. This carving process took only two tools, a chisel and a skew chisel. On a much smaller star, you could probably use just a knife as long as the wood was soft like basswood. Just like hand carved letters, the shadows created by the angled surfaces down to a center line give the carved star a very distinctive look.

MOUNTING THE BANNER

After gluing the flag and the staff together, blend in the joint and round over the straight end of the flag. Lay the banner on the eagle and determine where the screw holes need to be drilled. The surface of the eagle's right wing where the banner will rest may need to be carved down a little to create a good seat for the underside of the banner. Another screw attaches the staff where it makes good contact with the lower part of the wing, just under the head. Countersink these holes on the back side and attach the banner assembly to the eagle.

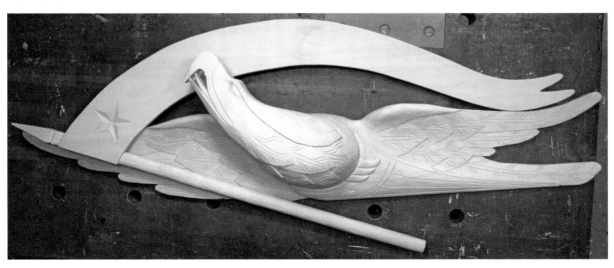

Completed eagle with banner.

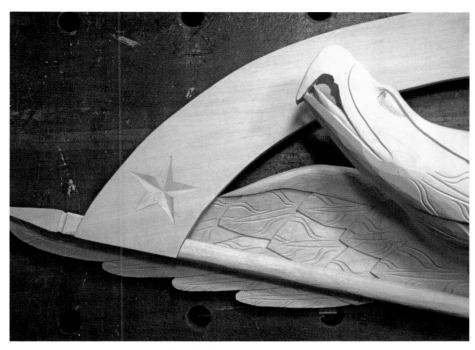

Detail of completed eagle.

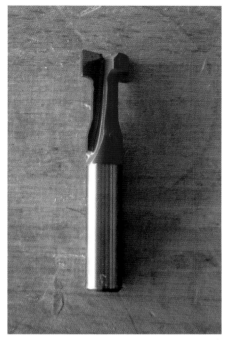

Key hole router bit.

The third attachment point is where the banner rests on the top edge of the eagle's left wing. I use a figure eight fastener that is traditionally used to mount roll top desktops to their bases. Any flat piece of steel or brass with two holes in it would work just as well as these brackets. The bracket is countersunk on the bottom to make it flush.

The carving is finished! I usually use a keyhole router bit to cut a pair of slots in the back of the carving to make a secure and hidden mounting. Just be sure that the wood is thick enough where you are going to plunge the bit in so that the bit doesn't come through to the front of your carving. To use the keyhole router bit, you first plunge it into the wood, then, holding it down, move the router towards the top of the piece. Move the router back and pull the bit out of the same hole that it went down into.

Key hole makes a great way to hang carving.

Chapter Seven
Finishing The Eagle

You have a few choices in how to finish your Bellamy style eagle. If you used mahogany or some other attractive hardwood for your eagle, you could use just a clear finish after painting the shield and banner. If the eagle is to be displayed inside, then lacquer is a good choice. If your eagle is going outside, then use a suitable outdoor finish such as outdoor oils or oil/varnish blends. Exterior paints should be used on the painted parts. Usually on basswood and pine, painting is the best option. Applying gold leaf is another finishing option.

The eagle shown here was carved out of basswood and finished with shellac. The shield was painted with acrylic paints. Painting the colors on the shield is made easier by the carved v-grooves that define the design. The entire piece was given two coats of amber shellac. After rubbing down the carving with a piece of crumpled brown paper (from a grocery bag) to smooth the surface, a van dyke brown glaze was applied with a brush then and wiped off. The glaze gets into the nooks and crannies and makes the details stand out. It also adds a little more color and gives the piece an aged appearance.

Painting Your Eagle

If the carving is to be entirely painted, begin by applying a coat of primer. If a water-based primer is used, the surface will have to be rubbed down after it is applied to smooth the surface. Note the location of the staff-mounting hole in the photo. The entire carving is then given a coat of water-base off-white paint. Exterior latex house paint works great and will hold up outside. Artist acrylic paint is used on the shield as well as for the lettering on the banner. The star on the banner is painted with gold leaf paint. Real gold leaf could be used for a brighter effect on the star. The small carved star on the shield is treated the same. The pupil and sometimes the tongue are painted red.

To add some color, take the brightness off of the white, and give an aged appearance, a van dyke glaze was applied and rubbed off. To seal everything, a coat of satin lacquer was sprayed on. If your eagle is going outside, topcoat with varnish instead of the lacquer.

Eagle finished with acrylic paint and shellac.

Detail of eagle.

Brush on primer.

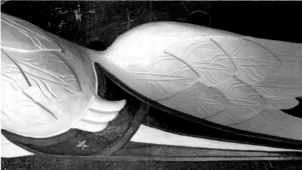

Red, white and blue painted shield.

Painted eyes and tongue.

Completed eagle.

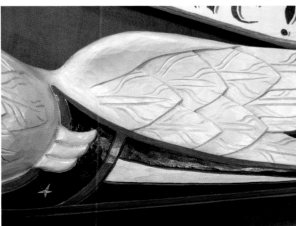

Completed eagle shield and talons.

Gold star on banner.

Head detail.

Chapter Eight

Carving a Pilot House Eagle

A Bellamy style pilot house eagle.

As steel replaced wood as the primary construction material for the ships on the seas, the demand for carved ornamentation on the outside of the ships was reduced. Wooden figureheads were no longer practical, but ornamentation did not disappear entirely. A big change associated with the conversion from sail to steam was the location of the pilot's wheel. It was moved forward, from the quarterdeck near the stern of the ship towards the bow. A wheelhouse or pilothouse was built to offer protection from the wind and sea. To give it an appearance of importance, the pilothouse was often decorated on top with a spread-winged eagle. These birds were carved in the round and often finished in gold leaf. They were either perched on a carved stone base or a ball.

The pilot house eagle that we will carve in this book is my design. It bears a strong resemblance to Bellamy's Lancaster figurehead eagle, but is perched on a ball like the pilothouse eagle shown in Chapter 1. The eagle carved on a ball was symbolic of America's strong presence in the world.

We will use basswood for this eagle. Begin by machining a piece that measures 3-1/2" x 3-1/2" x 18" long. Transfer the pattern to it with a piece of carbon paper. The grain will run in the same direction as the beak and the tail feathers. Part of the ball will not fit on this piece, so another block will be glued on later. On the table saw, make a 45-degree bevel cut on each top corner. This cut needs to produce a good machined surface. A band saw should not be used because the flatness of this surface will determine the quality of the joint later with the wings. Save the cut off pieces.

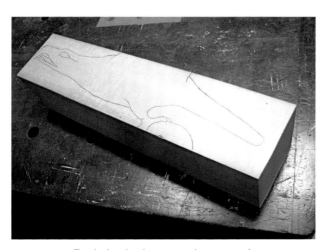

Eagle body drawn on basswood.

Block with 45 degree bevels.

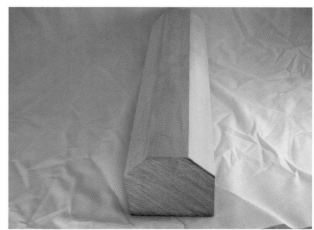

Bevels cut with table saw.

Apply small beads of glue.

Temporarily re-attach triangular pieces.

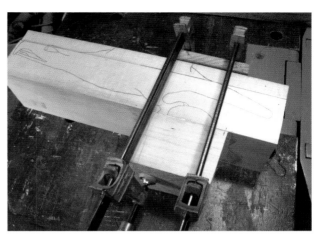

Glue on extra wood for ball.

Place a drop of instant glue on the each end of the freshly sawn bevel and reattach the sawn off triangle. The piece has some of the drawn pattern on it that we will need when we saw out the blank. But before we can saw out the blank, we have to glue on a block that is the same thickness and is wide enough for the rest of the ball that didn't fit on the original block. Clamp the two pieces and allow enough time for the glue to set up. Draw the rest of the pattern then take the assembled piece to the band saw.

Bandsaw out the blank using a 1/4" wide blade. I decided to leave a little bit of extra wood next to the legs of the eagle. Most of the carv-

ing will be done with the ball in a vise and I felt more comfortable with the added strength since this area has some cross grain. This area is marked with two X marks in the photo.

A great deal of this project is "design as you go." It is often difficult to draw a pattern in two dimensions and get a good feeling of how multiple parts will come together in proper scale in three dimensions. I cut out three different variations of a wing on foam board and held each one up to the eagle until I could decide which one was the best size and shape. I then traced this board onto a piece of basswood that was 1-1/2"thick.

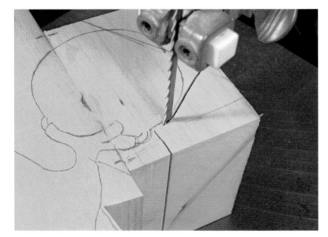

Cut out the body and ball with bandsaw.

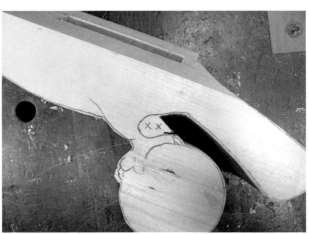

Extra wood was left at 'X' for strength.

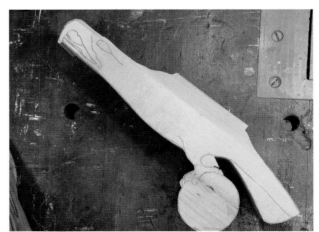

The sawn out blank.

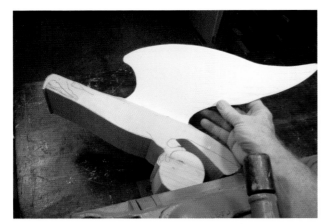

Hold wing pattern next to body to check for proper proportion.

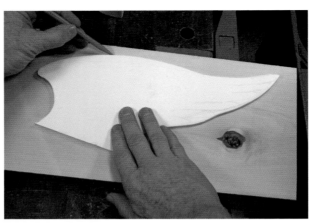

Lay out wing blanks from 1-1/2" thick stock. Grain should run in the direction of the long wing feathers.

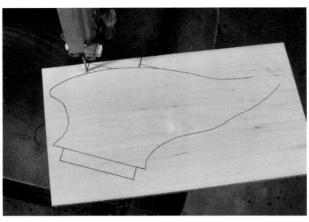

Saw out wings on bandsaw. Extra wood was left for two gluing pads and tenon.

Before you saw out the wings, draw two gluing pads on the top of the wings and a 3/4" wide tenon on the bottom. Note that the upper blade guard on the band saw is way too high. This was done just for the photograph and was set at the proper height during the sawing. The blade guards should always be close to the wood being cut for safety and to offer support for the blade during the cut. The tenon should be 1/2" shorter than the wing on each side. Stay just off of the drawn line with the saw cut. Save some of the waste that has a straight edge.

A 12" disc sander is used to sand the wood up to the drawn line on the tenon. Be sure to make this surface perfectly parallel to the original straight line of the wing. The tenon will be 3/8" thick. I marked it on the end of the tenon with a marking gauge. This is not really necessary but I do it mostly to help set up the table saw.

I cut the tenons to their proper thickness on the table saw. A router table could also be used and, in fact, is probably a safer way to do it. Use some of the scrap pieces from the wing as practice pieces to set the saw blade to the right height to get a 3/8" thick tenon. On the

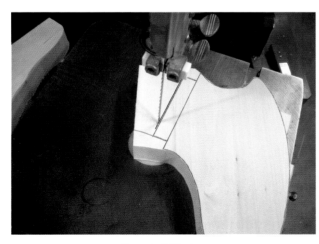

Saw out tenon.

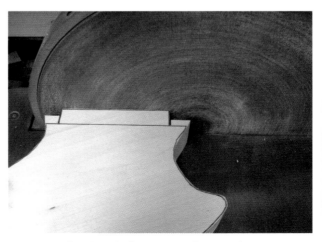

Sand end of tenon on disc sander.

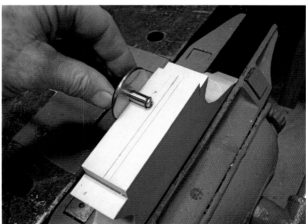

Layout tenon with marking gauge.

Cut tenon on table saw.

Cut tenon 3/4" long and 3/8" thick.

Cut tenon shoulders on bandsaw.

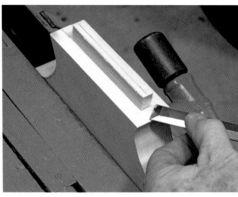

Use chisel to clean up shoulders.

table saw, you have to focus on applying steady pressure of the short length of the tenon to the fence. Saw one side, turn it over and saw the other side and the tenon will be in the exact center of the board. It is better to have the thickness just a hair over 3/8" rather than under. Note that a sacrificial fence is attached to the actual table saw fence. This allows the tenon to be cut all the way to its edge.

Use the band saw to cut the tenon so that it is 1/2" shorter than the wing on each end. Clean up the cut with a chisel so that the shoulders of the tenon are perfectly flat.

Layout the mortise in the body of the eagle. The body can be clamped in the pattern makers vise and adjusted so that the 45-degree flat surface is level with the floor. This is done just to make it visually easier to cut the mortise straight. The mortise is cut with a 3/8" mortising chisel to a depth of just over 3/4".

Some adjusting of the mortise with a flat chisel may be needed to get a good fit. The tenon should fit into the mortise snugly. Dry assemble the three pieces and admire your work up to this point but do not glue the wings to the body yet.

Layout mortise.

Adjust tilting vise so that the beveled surface is level.

Cut mortise with 3/8" mortising chisel.

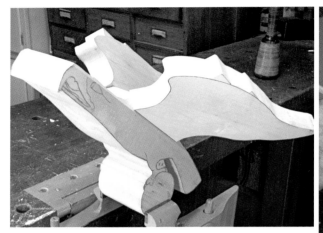

Test fit the joints.

Draw center line around the body of the eagle.

Drill out open areas of beak.

Saw off some waste beside beak.

Take the assembly apart and draw a center line on the body. The centerline is a reference to help you carve off wood symmetrically. Drill some holes through the open spaces of the beak. Then take the body to the band saw and saw off some waste from both sides of the beak.

The wings have quite a bit of contour to them. A lot of the waste that has to come off to get this shape will be carved off before the wing is glued on. Either clamp the wing to the workbench or hold it in the vise and use a gouge to carve off the waste. A drawknife can be used to shave off some wood from the outside of the wing tip. Now the wings are ready to be glued on to the body.

Draw curve on edge of wing.

Carve out inside of wing.

Carve outside of wing with drawknife.

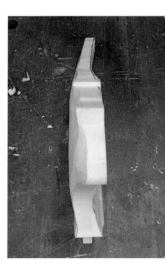

Curvature of wing.

Spread glue on surfaces of mortise and tenon.

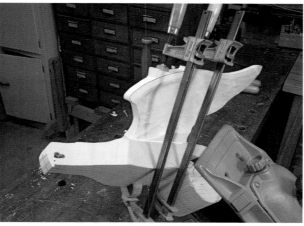

Pull the joints together with a pair of clamps for each wing. You can only clamp one wing at a time.

Both wings in place.

Spread some woodworkers glue on all of the surfaces of the mortise and the tenon. Apply clamps and check to make sure that the wings are seating properly and that a small amount of glue is being squeezed out of the joint. Now you can really see the purpose of the gluing pads that were added to the outline of the wings. The outer edges of the wings are curved and the clamps would otherwise slide off. The clamps rest on these pads on one end and on the opposite corner of the body on the other.

Wait until the next day to start carving on the assembled eagle. This allows the glue to cure fully. The first thing to do on the wings is to remove the clamping pads with a gouge. Use a variety of gouges to blend in the wings to the body. It is much easier to see how the wings need to be contoured now that they are attached.

The tail feathers will taper into the body in the shape of a fan. Draw this on the wood and use a gouge to remove the wood on each side where the tail meets the body. The tail feathers themselves will form

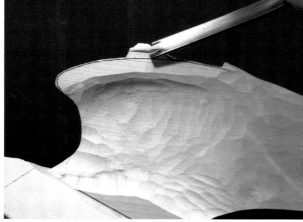

Cut off glue pads.

Blend joints.

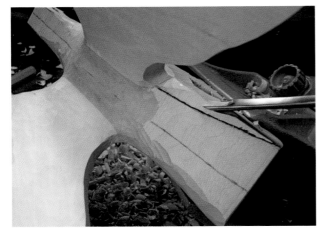

Shape tail.

Carve curve in tail feathers with drawknife.

Carve underside of tail.

an arc. Remove the excess wood on the top of the tail feathers with a small drawknife and underneath with a large #6 gouge.

Here are a couple of views showing the shape of the wings. They are convex on the top and concave on the undersides. Like all of Bellamy's eagles, there is a shadow created by the concavity of the inside top edges of the wings.

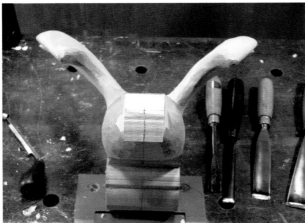

The eagle is taking shape. Front view.

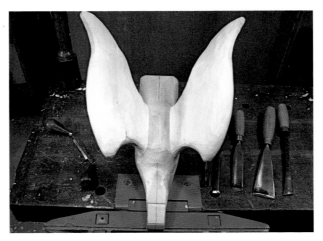

Top view. Note shape of wings.

Chapter Nine
Adding the Details From Head to Tail

The head on this pilot house eagle is carved much the same way as the head on the eagle in Chapter 5. The obvious exception is that this eagle has both sides of the head carved. So now the challenge becomes carving both sides symmetrically. If this is your first carving of an eagle in the round, then proceed carefully. If, on the other hand, you have carved a few Bellamy eagles, then it becomes pretty routine. Here is where the center line that was drawn earlier is a big help to use as a reference

Begin by drawing out the eye and beak details. Use a v-tool to outline the beak and the eye. The carved line on the bottom edge of the eye continues to the top of the head to form a feather just like in the previous eagle.

Round over the eye with a back bent gouge. A skew chisel is used to clean out the corners. The pupil is formed with a #7 gouge. Carve away the wood in front of the pupil so that it can be seen from a front view. The brow should figure prominently above the eye.

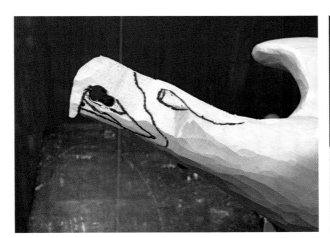

Draw eyes and beak.

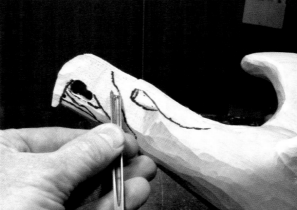

Use V-tool to carve edge of beak.

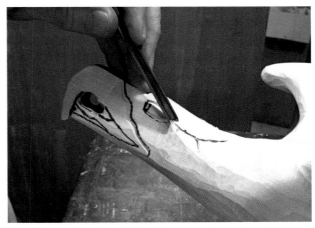

Use V-tool to carve outline of eye and continue the cut to form a feather on the back of the head.

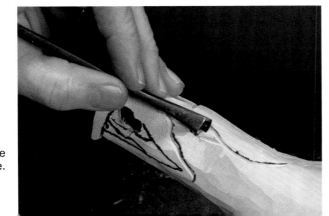

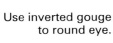

Use inverted gouge to round eye.

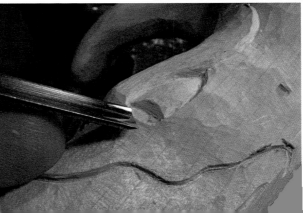

Carve pupil and remove wood from in front of the eye with a #7 gouge.

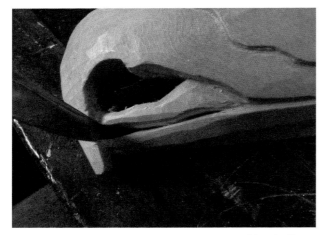

Cut out small areas around the tongue with a knife.

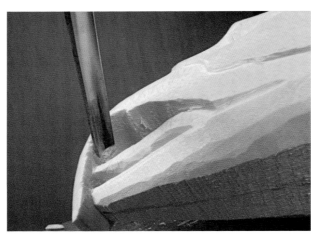

Clean up the inside of the beak with a gouge.

The finished head.

Use a coping saw to cut out the open space in the beak. Shape the tongue with a knife and clean up the inside of the beak with a gouge. The beak should taper down to about 1/4" in the front and the edges are left square. Be sure to remove all of the band saw marks and leave all surfaces carved with very shallow facets.

A lot of wood needs to be removed on the neck region so that it flows nicely from the body to the head. You can use either a drawknife, a large flat gouge, or a knife to do this.

Next we will switch our focus to the other end of the eagle, the tail. Start by drawing one feather in the center of the top side. This feather will lay on top of the others. Then draw three feathers on each side of this center one. About 1/3 of each of these feathers is covered by the feather that is on top of it. Begin carving them with a v-tool cut along the lines that you drew. Use a #3 gouge to remove the wood from the surfaces of the feathers to create a layered effect. We will come back to detail them and to carve the underside of these feathers later.

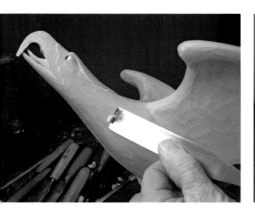

Taper the neck with a gouge...

...or with a knife.

Draw seven tail feathers. Carve on the line with a v-tool.

Layer the top of the feathers with a # 3 gouge.

Chapter 10
Carving the Wing Feathers.

When you are happy with the shape and the thickness of the wings, you can start drawing on the feathers, beginning with the underside of the wing. We are going to design the feather layout right on the wing. It could not be done on paper effectively since the wing is so curved. By dividing the wing into sections and then filling in those sections with a certain number of feathers, the two wings will come out looking the same. Start by drawing three lines as shown in the photograph. One group of feathers, the primaries, are much longer than the rest. The next two groups are roughly the same length. Draw in the primary feathers followed by two rows of secondary feathers. Try not to make all of the feathers line up with the feathers in the next row; stagger them as best you can. Fill in the remaining space with much smaller feathers.

Use a coping saw to saw out the waste around the wing tips.

Use a v-tool to cut along all of the lines that you drew for the feathers. It really doesn't matter which end that you start with, just outline

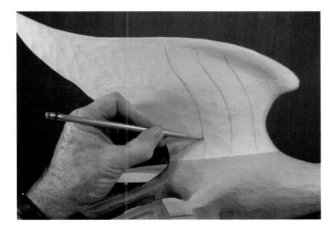
Draw four groups of feathers on inside of wing.

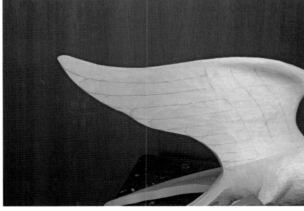
Draw primary feathers.

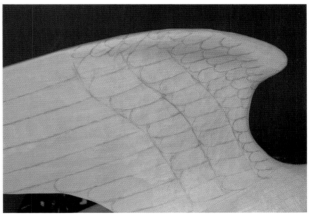
Fill in the other feather groups.

Saw out ends of feathers with a coping saw.

Start carving feathers with V-tool.

Carve all of the feathers with V-tool.

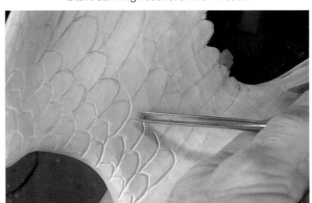

Make deep stop cuts in corners.

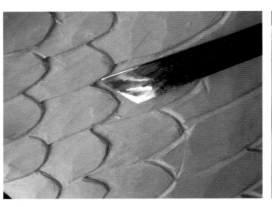

You can get into corners with a skewed gouge.

You can also cut the flat faces of the feathers with the skew gouge.

Or you can layer the feathers with a #3.

all of them at once. You could carve one feather completely at a time but that would be very inefficient. It is always best to carve with one tool first and carve everything that you can do with that tool before switching to another tool. Otherwise you spend too much time switching tools and not enough time carving.

A variety of tools are used in the layering of the feathers. Some of the smaller ones you can do with just a small #3 gouge. To get into the corners where three feathers come together, make a series of stop cuts with a knife. You can then remove the wood in these corners with the same knife or even better, a skewed gouge. The skewed gouge is also good for removing the wood from the face of the feathers. The side of the gouge next to the long tip can ride along the edge of the

adjacent, higher feather to help guide it. If you do not have a skewed gouge, a straight #3 gouge will work fine. Sometimes you have to go over areas a couple of times to get a clean, consistent layering effect. And, as always, it is important to have your tools sharp, especially in basswood.

Here is the almost complete underside of the left wing. Carve the right wing in the same manner. All that remains are the quills and the barbs.

Draw the quill as a double line that runs on the center of the feathers. The quills should come to a point just before the end of the feather. Carve along these lines with a v-tool. The barbs are also carved with the v-tool. They are carved in pairs and have an S shape. Start the

All of the feathers have been carved.

Drawing the quill.

Carving the center quills with a v-tool.

Carve the s-shaped barbs in pairs.

The completed underside of the right wing.

The completed underside of the left wing. Note the shadow created at the top of the wing.

cut running parallel to the quill, turn to the outside and finish by turning towards the tip of the feather. The intention is to simulate realism and not to be anatomically perfect. This is a tedious process but well worth the time spent.

The underside of the wings are finished!

On a true pilot house eagle, the top side of the wings were often either not carved at all or carved with very little detail. This is because they were going to be mounted high up on the top of the pilothouse and the top surfaces of the eagle would not be seen. The eagle being carved here is not going to live on top of a pilot house and the top

surfaces will more than likely be seen, so the details will be carved on both sides of the wings.

The feathers on the top sides of the wings are laid out differently than the underside. The wing is divided into six sections and filled in with feathers. Both wings are drawn at once, as well as the back of the eagle. Note that the feathers are layered in the opposite way than they were on the underside of the wings.

All of the feathers on the top of the body and wings are carved the same way as was done on the underside. They are first defined with the v-tool and then layered using a knife, a skew gouge and a flat

The basic feather groups drawn out on the top of the right wing.

The groups have been filled in with feathers.

Now all of the feathers on the tops of the wings have been drawn.

A spoon shaped v-tool is required to outline the feathers on the eagle's back due to the proximity of the wings.

The feathers on the top of the wings are carved in the same manner as those on the underside.

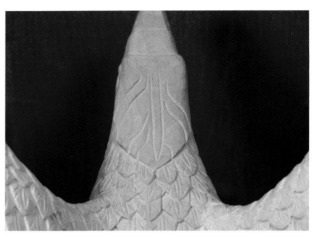

The large feather on the top of the head is treated just like the others. This feather originates at the eye.

gouge. The angle of the wings to the top of the body make it difficult to get to the feathers on the top of the body with a regular, straight shaft v-tool so a bent or spoon shape v-tool must be used.

Tip
Sharpening bent and spoon shaped carving tools is a little bit more difficult that straight ones. The outside bevel is ground and polished just like any other tool except that the angle is adjusted to compensate for the curve. It is the inside of the edge that is a challenge. Regular slip stones and strops just cannot get in there. This photo shows a 1"-inch diameter felt wheel that has been charged with abrasive compound being used to polish the inside edge of a small spoon shaped gouge.

Continue drawing and carving the feathers on the breast and sides of the eagle. Leave the feathers on the leg area for later, after the legs are shaped, in case some refinements are needed in these areas after the feet are carved. The large, single feather that is on top of the head can be treated in different ways. I chose to carve it just like the rest of the feathers.

The photo shows the side of the eagle with all of the feathers carved. It also shows the different shades of basswood that were used for the body and the wings. The body was made from Appalachian basswood and the wings were made from northern white basswood from Wisconsin. Since the growing season is shorter for the basswood trees grown in the northern parts of its range, the growth rings are usually much closer together. This gives the wood a finer texture than the southern variety.

Using a small felt wheel to hone the inside of a spoon v-tool. The edge of the felt wheel is tapered to fit the shape of the v-tool.

Side view of the eagle with almost all of the feathers completed. Note the two shades of basswood.

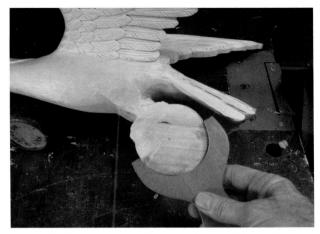

Jig for measuring the roundness of the ball.

Front view of the ball with the drawn legs and talons.

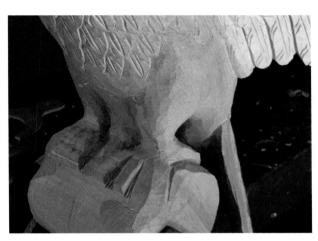

Start carving the talons.

With the eagle mostly complete, it is time to carve the talons and shape the ball. There are two issues with carving the ball. First, it is a challenge to get it perfectly spherical. And second, up to this point in the carving process, the eagle has been held steady for carving by clamping the ball in the vise. We are about to lose that luxury, so we will have to find another way to hold it. As for getting the ball round, I have made a jig that will help. The jig is simply a piece of 1/8" plywood that has a semicircular arc cut out that matches the shape of the ball. Use this aide and measurements to sketch in the ball from the front view. Also sketch the legs and talons.

Begin carving the talons with a v-tool and some small skews. Start shaping the legs as well. The idea here is to just visualize where the pieces go for now. Looking at the eagle from the front, I thought that it was a bit broad in the hips, so some wood needed to be removed on the side of the legs. This is why I didn't carve feathers on the legs yet.

Carving the ball has to be done carefully in order to get it as round as possible. I found that a wooden hand screw clamp that is clamped

Front view of the eagle so far.

Ball held in a handscrew clamp and then clamped to the workbench. Start rounding the ball from both sides.

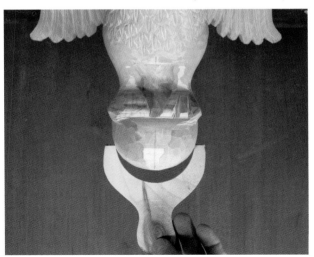

Checking the progress with the jig. The ball is not quite round.

Drill out space between legs.

Two drilled holes will help in carving out the space between the legs.

The space between the legs is taking shape.

to the bench did a good job of holding the ball. The body and wings of the eagle are hanging off of the workbench so make sure that it is secure. Use an inverted #3 gouge to shape the ball. Carve down to the center line that was drawn previously. Use the semicircular jig to check your progress. Here the ball looks close to being round but the jig says that it is still a little fat.

Put the ball back in the vise again, so that some holes can be drilled between the legs. Use pieces of leather to prevent the jaws of the vise from damaging the ball. Use a 3/8" drill bit to drill out a couple of holes. Look from both the side and front to make sure the holes are in the right spots. Also be careful when the drill bit comes out the other side that it doesn't continue forward and damage the underside of the tail.

The holes give you a start in carving out the waste between the legs. At this time the extra wood that was left behind the legs, to add strength while the body was carved, must be trimmed back. Continue to shape the ball, legs, and toes. You will find that some areas will be hard to reach with your regular tool collection, so now is the time to

The top of the ball is carved and the talons can be shaped further.

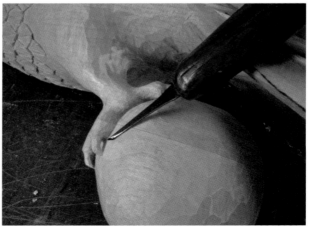

Use a very small (home made) skew chisel to carve out the space beneath the claws.

The completed ball and talons.

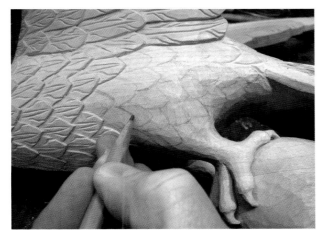

Draw out the remaining feathers on the body.

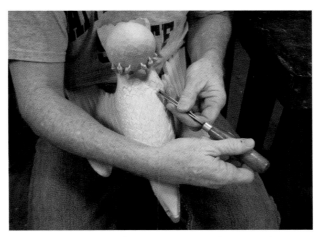

Sometimes you have to use your lap as a vise.

Using the spoon v-tool to get to the feathers behind the legs.

get out those odd shaped carving tools that you bought a long time ago but have never used.

The innermost toes are higher than the others because they are sitting closest to the top of the ball. In fact, the outermost toes are quite a bit lower than the inner ones.

The amount of detail that is carved on the talons is a matter of personal taste. In this case, they were carved without joints and a lot of detail. Very small gouges and a skew chisel were used to carve under the claws. Make sure that the toes are the same size and shape. Also, carve under them a little so that they appear to be resting on the ball, and are not part of it.

Now that the talons are carved, the remaining feathers on the body and legs can be carved. Draw the feathers on the legs, but only on the top part of them. The feathers are carved just like all of the previously carved feathers. Holding the carving is a challenge, now that the ball is completed. Your lap replaces the workbench. It is actually easy to hold the eagle steady with the wings cradling either one of your legs or your waist. The area between the ball and the tail feathers requires spoon gouges and whatever else will work in the confined space.

The legs require a scaly texture which could be carved or burned in with a suitable woodburning pen. This is definitely a departure from

Using a burning tool to apply texture the legs.

The talons are textured as well.

a traditional approach in the carving process, but it works too well to discount it. Cover the entire surface of the legs with burned scales and some random marks on the toes. The legs look unsightly now but the texture will be appreciated after they are painted.

A pilot hole must be drilled on the bottom of the ball for mounting. The location of this hole is critical. If it is drilled in the wrong spot, the eagle will not be right when it is mounted. If the front to back location is off, the eagle will either lean too far forward or stand too vertical. This could actually be off just a fraction and not spoil the look of the final mount. But if the hole is off to one side, the eagle will lean. It will be very noticeable because one wing will be higher than the other.

To accurately mark the front to back location of the hole, I placed a piece of carbon paper on the bench, facing up. I then held the eagle at the angle that I wanted and lowered it on to the carbon paper. By moving it slightly, a mark was made on the bottom of the ball at the exact spot that gives the carving the desired front to back angle. The eagle was then placed upside down on the drill press table with the wings resting firmly on the table. Since the shape of the wings would cause the carving to rock, a shim was placed under the wings to steady them. This whole assembly was moved around until the bottom of the drill bit was directly over the mark that was made by the carbon paper. The 5/16" hole was drilled about halfway into the ball.

The final step in the carving process is to add detail to the tail feathers. Once again, these are carved just like the rest of the feathers.

Using a drill press to drill the mounting hole in the ball.

The last feather group, the tail is detailed.

Chapter 11
Finishing the Pilot House Eagle

arted, a 23k gold leaf finish was planned. bject and finding out that there were some decision was made to paint it instead. ing process is sanding the surface where lly do not sand my carvings but in some rtant to do a thorough job of the sanding surface where the carving facets are only g is rarely acceptable.

ly mounted on a block so that two hands /s are the only parts of this carving that ip of flexible, cloth back sandpaper was in sanding the ball. The gold, aluminum por works very well for sanding any con- y machine. A very narrow strip, about a er the claws and worked back and forth The rest of the ball, which could not be dpaper, was sanded by hand with a piece of folded sandpaper. Start sanding with P180 grit and work your way up to P320 grit.

The claws are very small and cross-grained so there is a potential for future damage from accidental rough handling. To help strengthen them, they were soaked with thin cyanoacrylate glue. Enough coats were applied so that no more adhesive would soak in. When the glue was fully cured, the claws were sanded with P600 grit sandpaper.

The final step in preparing the surface for painting is to very lightly sand the feathers all over the carving with a mini sanding mop (also from Klingspor). The goal here is to very lightly soften the sharp edges, not to sand the surface. The P320 grit sanding mop is held in a flexible shaft rotary tool.

A water base white primer was applied with brushes. A small flat brush was bent so that it could reach the areas behind the ball. The rest of the carving was painted with a wider flat brush. Make sure that every carved detail is coated with primer.

A very narrow strip of sandpaper is inserted under the claws to sand and further round them.

The sanding of the ball is finished and the claws are coated with thin cyanoacrylate glue to make them harder.

A small sanding mop is used to smooth any sharp edges.

A small bent paint brush is used to get primer onto hard to reach areas.

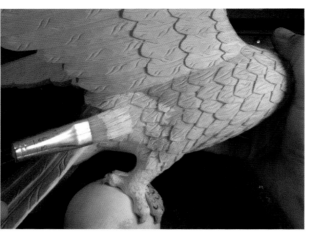

A larger brush is used on the larger areas.

A piece of crumpled brown paper bag is used to rub out the primed surface to make it smooth.

The water-based primer will raise the grain on the wood. This surface must be smoothed before the topcoat is applied. A crumpled piece of brown paper bag works great for this purpose. It is abrasive enough to do the job, but gentle enough so that no paint is removed. Just make sure that there is no printing on the paper, because the ink will rub off on the carving.

The ball was painted with an acrylic antique blue paint. Two coats were required. The entire surface of the eagle was painted with a gold leaf paint. This paint is oil-based and intended for interior use. There is an exterior grade gold leaf paint available, but it is not as bright as the interior paint. This paint contains copper compounds and it will mellow with time. Two coats are required.

The only other places that are painted are the pupils and the tongue. The pupils are painted white with a dark grey center. The tongue is painted red. All acrylic painted surfaces dry to a dull finish, so they were given a coat of semi-gloss lacquer applied with a brush.

Apply two coats of gold leaf paint.

The tongue is painted red, and the iris of the eye is painted white with a dark gray center.

The eagle is mounted with a lag screw through the base into the ball.

The mahogany base for the pilot house eagle is made in two parts. The pieces were turned on the lathe from two-inch stock. The top piece has a small cup turned on top that matched the bottom of the ball. This will give the carving a secure foundation. A countersunk hole is drilled through the top base section. The ball is attached to the top base section with a 3/8" thick lag screw. The top section of the base is attached to the bottom section with three screws. This base gives the eagle a very solid support.

Some Final Photos

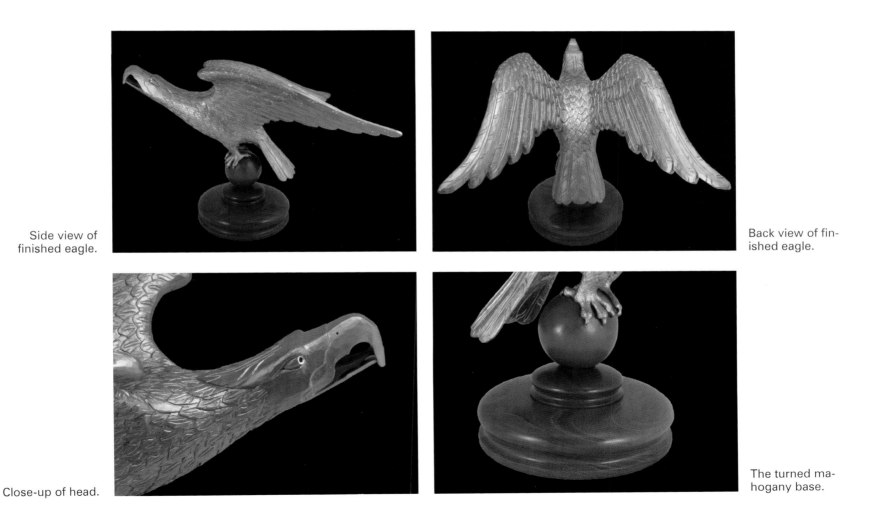

Side view of finished eagle.

Back view of finished eagle.

Close-up of head.

The turned mahogany base.

Chapter 12

Carve a Bellamy Soaring Eagle

This style of eagle by Bellamy is very different than his spread winged eagles. It is still very recognizable as one of his carvings, due to the classic head style and the treatment of the eye and feathers.

The project shown here will be simplified from the Bellamy eagle shown in Chapter 1. The feet and arrow will be left off.

Enlarge the pattern to whatever size you want, transfer it to the wood, and saw it out on the band saw. It is not necessary to draw all of the lines on the wood, since they will be ꞏ this case, the basswood blank was 10" w To help in the carving process, a few hꞏ spaces of the beak. The blank was then with a couple of screws from the backsideꞏ what would be the center line of the bodꞏ here, so there is little danger of hitting thꞏ backer board was then clamped securely

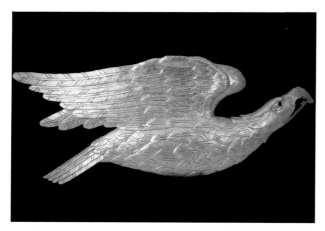

Bellamy style soaring eagle with gold leaf finish.

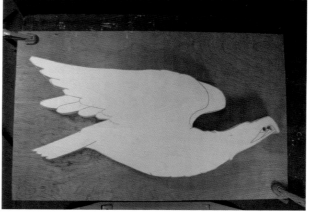

The sawn out blank fixed to backer board.

Begin rꞏ

Take the wings down to about 1/2".

With large shallow gouge, smooth the surface.

Use a large smoothing
up the body.

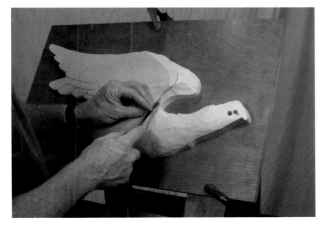

Using a carving stand to take strain off back.

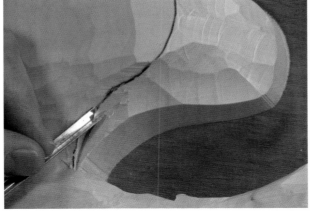

Define the bottom wing.

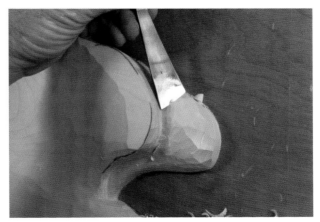

Round over the bottom wing.

Begin to remove waste material with a large, fairly deep gouge. A #8 sweep that's about 1-1/4" to 1-1/2" wide works well. Use a mallet to drive the tools and take off a lot of wood from the wings and around the body. One of the high spots on this carving will be at the top of the upper wing, so be sure to leave the wood high here. There is a hollow area just below this high spot that creates a shadow under the wing.

Deep gouges remove wood quickly but leave a coarse texture. Remove the coarse texture with a large, nearly flat, #3 gouge. The rough carving is complete, leaving just the details.

When working on a flat carving such as this one, the roughing out is done while standing and with the carving piece clamped flat on the bench. However, when detail carving is done, while the piece is flat on a bench, you tend to lean over the bench which is very hard on your back. At this stage, I prefer to clamp the carving on an inclined stand so that the work is right in front of me and I don't have to lean over. I can then either carve while standing on a cushioned mat or sitting on an adjustable chair. The carving stand is made from three panels that are hinged together so that they fold up for easy transport and storage.

Only the front shoulder and the tips of the longest feathers of the back wing show from behind the front wing. The front shoulder is carved by simply dropping it down to about a third of the thickness of the wood with a v-tool and a flat gouge. It is rounded off in front. Undercut the top wing slightly to create a shadow over the bottom wing.

The head on this eagle is carved in the same manner as the other heads in this book. There are a few differences in the details. One is that there is a hood separating the head from the body. And another is that the tongue is shorter and does not extend out to the upper mandible.

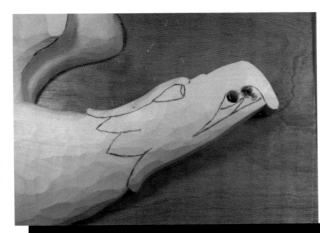

Holes are drilled in the beak open spaces.

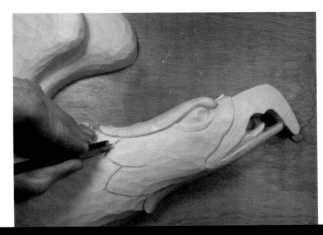

The head is carved just like other Bellamy eagle carvings.

All of the feathers drawn.

Using a relief carving knife.

A re

The feathers are drawn out according to the pattern. They are carved just as before, except that I am using a relief carving knife to put stop cuts in the corners.

There are times when a knife is a great tool to use in relief carving. But the only problem with using a knife on flat work is the lack of control. Because the handles of most knives are only big enough for one hand, that hand must do three things on its own. It must guide the cut and apply the driving force of the cut, but at the same time "apply the brakes" to avoid a costly follow-through slice. By making the handle long enough for both hands, these tasks are divided between two hands instead of just one. This results in a strong, but safe, well guided cut. I designed this 11-inch long knife with a depression on the end of the handle for the thumb.

Once all of the feathers are carved, carve the quills and barbs with a v-tool just as before.

HOW TO APPLY G

Gold leaf may be considered the ultin lamy eagle. Your carving will be covered i or tarnish. As long as it is not handled ro it will last indefinitely.

Metal leafing comes in a variety of for silver, copper or a mixture of these and oth called composition gold leaf or Dutch met all but a mixture of brass, copper and zinc of genuine gold leaf, but it will tarnish ove tation gold leaf may be prolonged by app

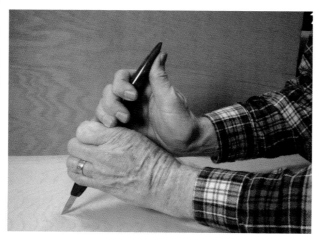

Using a relief carving knife with two hands for total control.

will send the sheet flying. There is another form of gold leaf called patent leaf where the gold is attached to a sheet. Since the gold stays attached to the paper until it is transferred, it is not subject to breezes. It is designed to be used outside, such as on a window, and is not practical for applying to a carved surface.

There are a few tools required for working with gold leaf. All of the tools are available from online sources and some can be made in the shop to save some money. The most important tool is a guilders brush. It is used to pick up the gold sheets and lay them down onto the prepared surface where it will adhere. The brush is two to four inches wide and consists of a double row of squirrel hair bristles. I used a 2" wide brush here. The gold sheets may be applied whole, but sometimes it is much more efficient to cut them into pieces. You may purchase a guilders knife and a pad to do this but a slightly sharpened spreader or table knife from the kitchen works just as well. The pad

can be made by stretching chamois cloth over a piece of wood. A very soft bristle artist's brush is needed to polish the gold after it has been applied.

Before the gold leaf is applied, the surface must be prepared. The wood needs to be slightly sanded to soften any sharp edges and then primed with a suitable primer. It is then painted. I used gold leaf paint on this carving thinking that if there were any small places that did not get completely covered in gold, they would show less than if a different colored paint was used instead.

Next a sizing is applied. The sizing can be either oil-based or water-based. Before the sizing is fully cured, it will be tacky. The window of opportunity, when the sizing is just the right tackiness for applying the leaf, varies. Oil-based sizing can take up to 12 hours to reach the ideal state, but the advantage is that the window of time is very long so it is used on large projects. Water-based sizing can be ready to guild in 30 minutes and can remain tacky for an hour or more.

Priming the finished carving.

Brushing on a base coat of gold paint.

Brushing on the gold leaf sizing.

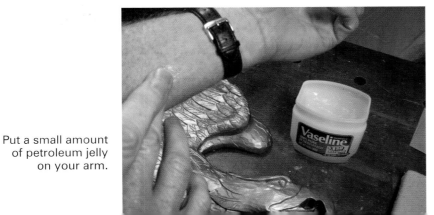

Put a small amount of petroleum jelly on your arm.

Transfer a very small amount of the petroleum jelly to the guilders brush.

Gently pull a sheet of gold onto the pad.

Cut a piece of gold leaf with knife.

Lay the gold sheet onto the prepared surface.

The water-based sizing is milky white in appearance when it is brushed on and turns clear when it is ready for the gold. The brush needs to be washed out with soap and warm water right away. When the sizing is ready, it may be difficult to tell which surface has been coated and which has not. It is best to work systematically so that you can keep track of what has been coated.

When the sizing is clear, it is ready for the gold. In very low humidity conditions, there may be enough static electricity in the guilders brush to pick up a gold sheet. Another technique is to use a small amount of petroleum jelly on the brush that will lift the leaf. Smear some of the jelly on your forearm and then pick up some on the brush. Do not use too much; just a little goes a long way.

The gold leaf book is held near the cutting pad and opened to expose a gold sheet. The brush is very gently brought into contact with the leading edge of the sheet and pulled onto the pad. With the brush held motionless, use the knife to slice a strip of leaf. The whole sheet could also be lifted without cutting if the target area is large enough. The brush and gold slice should be moved with caution so that it does not fall off of the brush. Lay the gold down on the free edge and then the end held by the brush. It is imperative that the sheet be laid down gently and not pulled or it will rip. I found that if the sheet is laid down loosely over the feathers there is some excess gold that can be worked into the carved details.

Cut small pieces of gold for small areas and to fill in.

Use a smaller brush to transfer small pieces of gold.

Small pieces of gold captured in a box lid will be used to fill in details.

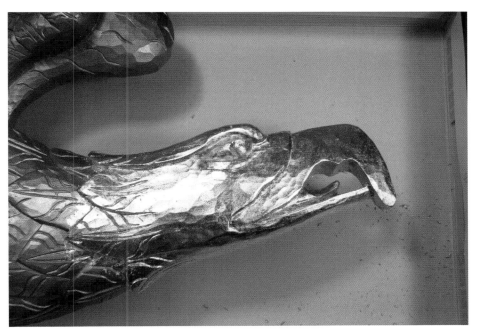

The head took six sheets of gold to cover.

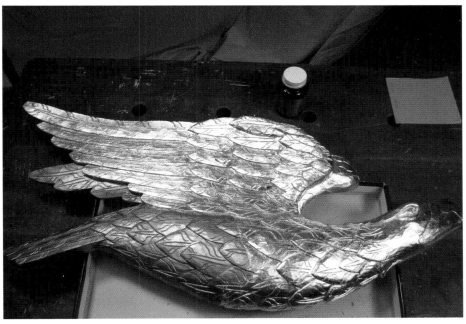

An entire book of 25 sheets of gold leaf were required to cover about 2/3 of the carving.

Small pieces of gold can be cut and maneuvered with a smaller brush. These small pieces are required in places like inside of the beak. A small box lid is placed under the part of the eagle that is being gilded in order to catch the small, loose pieces of gold that fall. These small pieces can be brushed into tight areas and along the carved grooves to fill in those spots that the larger sheets of gold did not adhere to.

It took six sheets of gold leaf to cover the head of the eagle. An entire book of 25 sheets covered about two thirds of the carving.

The gold leafing process continues until all surfaces have been covered. Several areas will undoubtedly be found that were missed by the sizing and will need to be coated and gilded. Changes in elevation of the carving and the edges are places that can be easily missed. Paint the eye and tongue red to complete the finish.

The gold may be left just as it is or coated with a clear finish. It may also be glazed to achieve an antiqued look.

The eye and tongue are painted red.

Chapter 13
Gallery

Eagles have always been such a popular subject for sculptors and wood carvers and will probably continue to be. I have had the occasion to carve a lot of them over the years. Not all of them have been Bellamy style eagles. Here are just a few.

Mahogany Bellamy eagle with a 12 foot wing span. Two pieces of 3" thick mahogany were used.

A 36" long mahogany Bellamy eagle. Photo taken on a sand dune near the beach.

An original adaptation of a Bellamy eagle. It is 36" long and carved out of basswood.

36" long Bellamy eagle with a draped flag on a staff. Painted basswood.

A 36" long basswood Bellamy eagle that is painted with gold leaf paint. *Photo courtesy of David Keller.*

Close-up view of the chestnut eagle.

A 72" long Bellamy eagle that is carved out of American Chestnut. The wood which was nearly wiped out by a blight in the 1920s, was recycled from old timbers that were used in a structure in the North Carolina mountains.

An early eagle carving carved out of basswood.

Mahogany eagle with 48" wingspan. I carved a pair of these for an entrance sign for a business park. They were painted with a sign painters enamel gold leaf paint.

Eagle holding carving tools with a scroll below. I used this as my logo and business sign for years. Note the similarity to the eagle with arrows shown on page 65.

A 12" tall miniature, military style, carousel horse. It is decorated with a Bellamy style eagle holding an American flag.

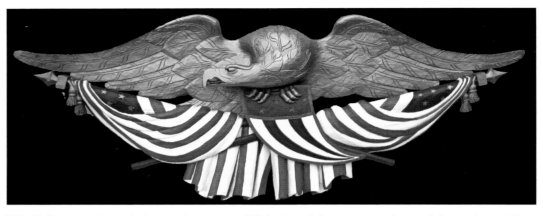

This Bellamy style eagle has a wing span of 60 inches. It is constructed out of three pieces. The two part eagle is carved much like any other eagle plaque. The flags, shield, and talons are on a separate piece that is attached with screws to the eagle. It is painted with acrylics and gold leaf paint. This project took approximately 100 hours to carve and paint.

A close up of the eagle with flags.

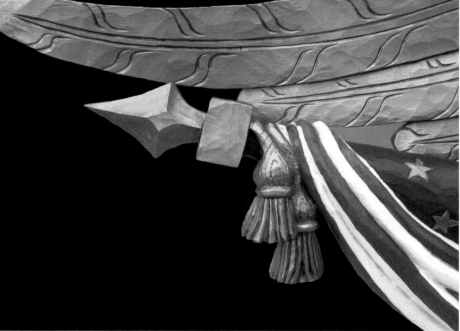

A detail photo showing the speared end of the flag staff and the tassels.

Chapter 14

Patterns

Bellamy Eagle Pattern

A popular Bellamy style eagle pattern. The pattern may be enlarged to any size that is desired although most of Bellamy's were 25" long. The carvings shown of this style in this book are 36" long

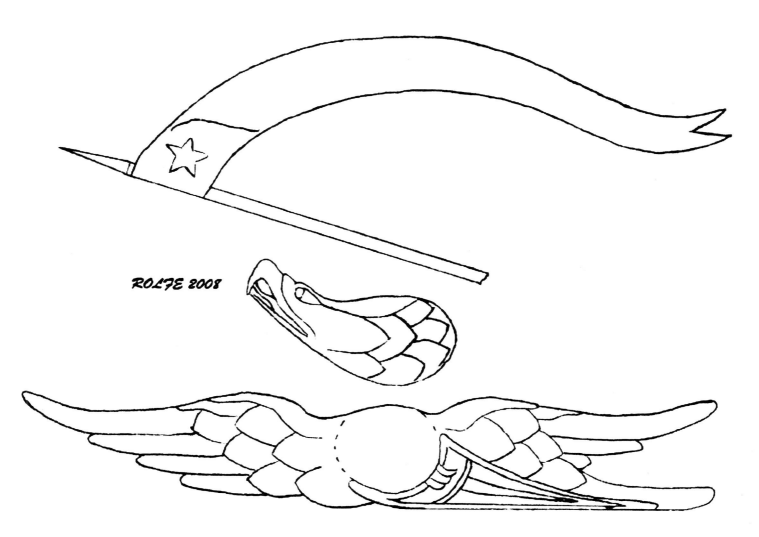

ROLFE 2008

Pilot House Eagle

The two part pattern for the pilot house eagle carved in this book. Feather layouts are omitted on the patterns because they would not be the same when transferred to the three dimensional carving.

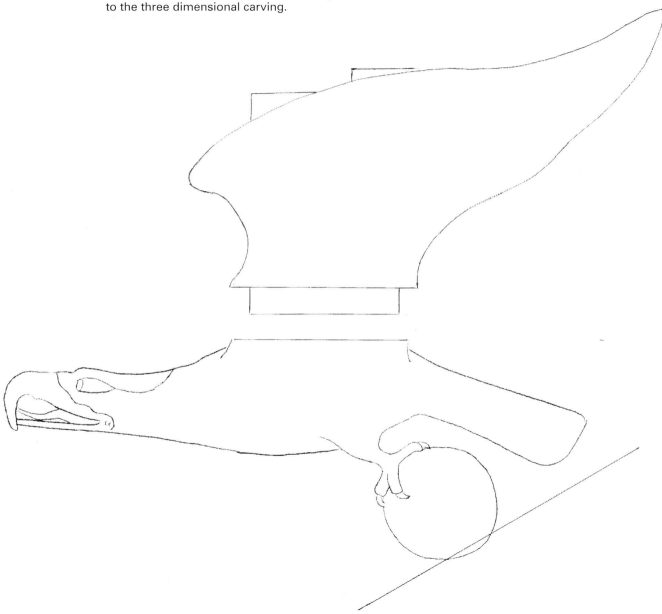

Soaring Eagle Pattern

Pattern for the soaring eagle. 10 x 24 x 2″

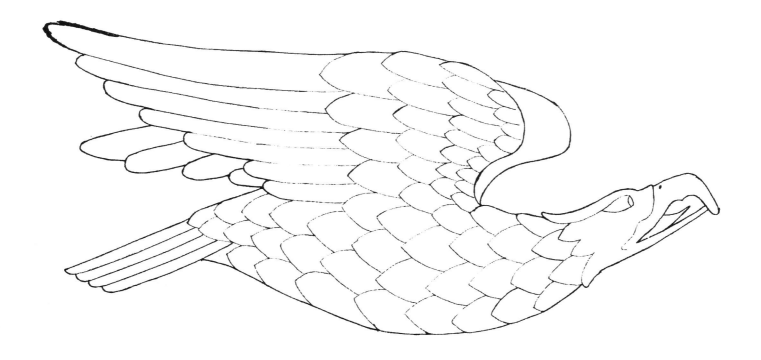

Two part pattern for the eagle shown in the Gallery chapter. The eagle is approximately 60 inches long.

Pattern for a soaring eagle by Bellamy. It is similar to the soaring eagle shown in chapter 1, page 12, and also the eagle that is carved in chapter 12 of this book. *Courtesy of Farnsworth Art Museum, Rockland, ME.*

Pattern for an eagle on a ball drawn by Bellamy. *Courtesy of Farnsworth Art Museum, Rockland, ME.*

Chapter 13
Bibliography

For more in depth information about John Haley Bellamy and other maritime wood carvers during the Golden Age of Wood Carving in America you may enjoy these books.

Brewington, M. V. *Shipcarvers of North America*. New York, NY: Dover Publications, Inc. 1972.

Fried, Frederick. *Artists in Wood, American Carvers of Cigar-store Indians, Show Figures, and Circus Wagons.* New York, NY: Bramhall House, 1970.

Hamilton, Georgia W. *Silent Pilots Figureheads in Mystic Seaport Museum.* Mystic, CT: Mystic Seaport Museum, Inc. 1984.

Sessions, Ralph. *The Shipcarver's Art, Figureheads and Cigar-store Indians in Nineteenth-Century America.* Princeton, NJ: Princeton University Press, 2005.

Smith, Yvonne Brault. *John Haley Bellamy Carver of Eagles.* Hampton, NH: Portsmouth Marine Society, 1982.